Living Our Faith After the Changes

EX LIBRIS
RICARDO C. CASTELLANOS

The Catholic Update Series:

Living Our Faith After the Changes

Explaining Catholic Thinking Since Vatican II

Edited by Jack Wintz, O.F.M.

Nihil Obstat:
Rev. John J. Jennings

Imprimi Potest
Rev. Andrew Fox, O.F.M.
Provincial

Imprimatur:
+Daniel E. Pilarczyk
Auxiliary Bishop of Cincinnati
July 22, 1977

The *Nihil Obstat* and *Imprimatur* are a declaration that a
book or pamphlet is considered to be free from doctrinal
or moral error. It is not implied that those who have granted
the *Nihil Obstat* and *Imprimatur* agree with the contents,
opinions, or statements expressed.

Cover Design by Michael Reynolds

SBN 0-912228-45-8

© 1977 St. Anthony Messenger Press
All rights reserved.
Printed in U.S.A.

CONTENTS

Introduction

You're strolling through the park and a strange black and
silver spacecraft lands near you. Immediately this foreign
object is threatening to you. And as pale green antpeople
descend from its trapdoor and stride toward you, you become
even more alarmed and fearful.

But they begin making friendly and gentle gestures. They
present you with a beautiful medallion and a box that plays
sweet music. They show you an album of photo-like portraits
of their families, their marriage customs and picnics back on
planet Skarmoc. They offer you fruit and what looks like
bread sticks. As you add up the many things you can experience in common with them, these creatures no longer seem
hostile.

Just because something is different doesn't mean it's harmful.

The purpose of this book—the third volume of the *Catholic
Update* series—is to show that the changes that have come
into the Church since Vatican II need not really be threatening to us. Yet, as we all know, these changes sometimes
come sailing into our lives like so many foreign objects and
it's not always easy to deal with them very comfortably.

Whose fault is that? Well, on the one hand it's partly our fault if we deliberately keep our distance and make no effort to understand these changes or to integrate them into our lives. Or the fault can lie in part with those in the teaching ministry of the Church. For they may have failed to take the time or the initiative to show that the changes in question are really friendly and benevolent to us—and that they are not that strange or foreign to our familiar Christian traditions and practice.

It's important therefore that we seek to *understand* the developments that have affected our Catholic faith in the past 20 years so that we can better *live* that faith. This collection of *Catholic Updates* is being published precisely to help in this task. Hopefully, as we grasp the rationale and explanations behind the changes in the Church's attitudes, in its liturgy, sacraments and devotions, we find that it's much easier to "get our act together" as practicing Christians.

This volume contains some of the most popular *Catholic Update* articles written to date and is dedicated to helping all of us in the Catholic community to harmonize our lives with our changing Church and world. In short, this book is designed to help us *live our faith after the changes*—as the title suggests—and to live it more fully and with more understanding.

Is the Church Going Soft?

by Mary Ann Deak

Is the Church sinking into a mushy permissiveness? It certainly is, we're tempted to exclaim. Just look around: confession lines are shorter; permission for mixed marriages and annulments seems easier to obtain; the "New Morality" extols individual conscience while Church leaders hesitate to lay down the law. No question—the Church is going soft!

And yet we know it's not fair to blame the Church for what is a wider cultural phenomenon. For example, it's not the Church that has urged fewer confessions. Under the impact of radio, TV, jets and satellites, the whole world has begun to change and to ask new questions, not only Catholics.

1

A Call to Adulthood?

Moreover, even though external things may appear too relaxed, many Catholic observers sense that an inner strength and maturity is growing in the Church. In his book *The People Are the Church* Father Eugene Kennedy proposes that the Catholic Christian community is growing more mature in its relationship to God.

Borrowing from the distinguished psychologist Gordon Allport, Father Kennedy contrasts the religion of childhood with mature religion. The religion of childhood is accepted on authority, imitates others, and is satisfied with outward expressions like words and rituals. Children believe in God because they have been told to do so by people they respect. Their prayers are usually ones that they've been taught to say by others either at home or at school. They are fascinated by ritual and are easily attracted to the symbols of the liturgy, just as they might make up "secret" gestures and passwords in their play. All of this is external to them—they probably do not perceive the deeper meaning underlying their beliefs, their prayers, their rituals. This is just what we expect of children, but of adults we expect greater maturity.

To be mature, Father Kennedy continues, "religious belief must be internalized and flow from the individual." As adults, we can no longer believe in God merely because someone tells us to do so—it must be our own sincere inner conviction. We cannot rely on rattling off rote prayers we learned as a child; prayer must become a real expression of our unique relationship with God. "The exercise of religion," says Vatican II, "consists before all else in those internal, voluntary, and free acts whereby man sets the course of his life directly toward God" (*Declaration on Religious Freedom,* #3).

The Church Is Growing Up

So maybe relaxing some rules and regulations hasn't happened because the Church has gone soft but because she has recognized and is demanding maturity in her members. As Vatican II acknowledged, "A sense of the dignity of the human person

2

has been impressing itself more and more deeply on the consciousness of contemporary man. And the demand is increasingly made that men should act on their own judgment, enjoying and making use of a responsible freedom, not driven by coercion but motivated by a sense of duty" (*Declaration on Religious Freedom*, #1).

A good parent realizes that young children need many rules, but as they approach adolescence, stress on rules gradually gives way to stress on inner responsibility. People cannot become responsible for themselves, making their own decisions freely, if someone else is forever standing behind them telling them what to do.

In the same way, the Church has taken a look at herself and realized that Christians should be growing more responsible in their commitment to their faith. They need the freedom to express that commitment as adults, in ways that will take into account their own unique relationships to God. Mature adults don't need lists of rules and regulations, especially if they are forced upon them rather than chosen freely, flowing from interior attitudes.

Salvation Means Religious Maturity

But are today's Christians really more mature? Are we really making responsible decisions and challenging ourselves to grow? Are we really seeking ways to grow closer to God or merely taking advantage of the relaxed rules and regulations? Ultimately, only individuals can answer such questions.

When the Friday abstinence law was done away with, our Church leaders urged us to continue some weekly self-denial. Have we? Fasting and prayer have been encouraged since the early days of the Church. Have we ever done any more than the bare minimum, with or without strict laws? Have we profited spiritually by confessing less or have we just put off facing our sinfulness? Greater freedom means greater responsibility, and if there is no corresponding growth on the inside, then we must ask ourselves if we are really responding to the Lord as he calls us from childhood to greater maturity.

Religious maturity is essential to salvation. According to Father Richard McBrien in *Has the Church Surrendered?*, there has been a growing understanding in recent years that the world is destined to partake of the Kingdom of God. Our participation in that final Kingdom, which is the meaning of salvation, will not be as *super*-humans but as perfect *human* beings. "Salvation is not liberation, but fulfillment. When man is fully man, that is, when man is everything God calls him to be, then salvation is at hand." Thus, growth as free and responsible persons is an important part of our being saved. It is only in this way that we can become the complete human beings God desires as the fulfillment of his creation.

Which Is Harder to Follow—Law or Conscience?

Many people, both inside and outside the Catholic Church, interpret the present trend as a breakdown in the authority of the Church. Father McBrien points out that this *authority-is-breaking-down* view "implies that the Catholic Church altered its style of moral teaching, not because of a legitimate development in its own critical self-understanding, but simply because it concluded that Catholics and non-Catholics alike would no longer accept that moral teaching." This view is wrong, he says, because what its promoters are disturbed about has to do with *cultural* non-essentials like Friday abstinence. They don't seem to notice that the central teachings of Jesus which are the life-blood of the Christian faith haven't changed in the slightest.

In fact, the gospel imperatives for social justice and peace are put forth more strongly than ever. How seriously do those Catholics who complain of a "soft" Church take recent encyclicals like *Populorum Progressio* (*On the Development of Peoples*) and *Pacem in Terris* (*Peace on Earth*)? Which is harder—to abstain from meat on Friday or to stand up for the black family who just moved into your all-white neighborhood? To cut down on what you eat during Lent or to refuse to buy produce at your favorite grocery store in support of a legitimate and justified boycott? Viewed in this way, it would appear that the Church is "harder" than ever.

Further, we are also forgetting that the Church has always taught that our conscience is our ultimate judge. Even an erroneous conscience must be obeyed! That's straight from the Baltimore Catechism. And Vatican II states that no one "is to be forced to act in a manner contrary to his conscience" (*Declaration on Religious Freedom*, #3). Of course, we all have a serious responsibility to form a good conscience and we are wise to turn to the guidance and authoritative teaching of the Church for that. But the rightness or wrongness of my individual action is determined by whether or not I acted in accord with my conscience. Understood in all of this, certainly, is my honest and genuine effort to learn the truth.

Scripture and Human Responsibility

What kind of laws and authority, then, do today's Christians need? John Giles Milhaven explores the Book of Genesis for a perspective on this matter. In *Toward a New Catholic Morality*, he reminds us that God made human beings to his image by sharing his dominion with them, as described in Genesis. "Let us make man in our image, after our likeness; and let them have dominion over the fish of the sea, and over the birds of the air, and over the cattle, and over all the earth, and over every creeping thing that creeps upon the earth" (Gen. 1: 26)

God, therefore, has given us responsibility for this world. Milhaven compares this sharing of dominion to a father who has turned his business over to his grown son. Of course, the father's presence means much to the son, and the father watches all that he does. But it is the son who is responsible— it is he who must make the decisions.

The Christian today, then, stresses more and more this positive obligation in his attitude toward law and authority, rather than certain negative patterns of the past. We still need laws and guidelines, of course; it is still possible to fool ourselves if we rely too much or solely on private conscience. We need the Church to teach us traditional values and set forth clear norms and guidelines. But sometimes general principles are needed more than specific directives. Each of us may have to

5

decide what those concrete things are that we must do in a
given situation.

We Need the Teaching Church

In the formation of their consciences, the Christian
faithful ought carefully to attend to the sacred and
certain doctrines of the Church. The Church is, by
the will of Christ, the teacher of the truth. It is her
duty to give utterance to, and authoritatively to
teach, that truth which is Christ himself, and also
to declare and confirm by her authority those
principles of the moral order which have their
origin in human nature itself (*Declaration on Religious Freedom*, #14).

Is this another cop-out? Doesn't this leave things too vague to
place any real demands on an individual? Not so, continues
Milhaven, for sharing God's dominion means it's up to us to
take action in regard to the world's problems, whether they
are on a global scale, like starvation in India or hate in the
American ghettos, or on a personal level, like the loneliness
of a senile mother, or our own indifference to religious practice. "Thinking along new lines, [today's Christian] lacks
certain 'outs' possible under the old morality. He cannot evade
his responsibility by saying that it is not clear what exactly he
is obliged to do. If he does not know what that something is,
then it's up to him to find out," writes Milhaven.

Such responsibility is in line with our ideas about the mature
Christian. The more seriously we take our obligation to care
for this world in all its aspects, the closer we come to the fullness God intended when he created us "to have dominion. . .
over all the earth." And, as St. Thomas Aquinas points out,

6

the greatness of God's power can be seen precisely because he can share so much of it with his creatures. The greater a creature is, the greater its Creator must be.

Jesus, the Servant

Jesus' way of exercising authority manifests the great respect he has for human freedom and an individual's inner responsibility. Reading through the Gospels, we are struck by the fact that he never used force. He simply proclaimed the truth and left his listeners free to accept or reject it, free to consider whether they would make it a part of their lives or not.

In the story of the rich young man, we hear him extend his invitation to "leave all and follow me," but he allows the young man to make his own decision, even though it means letting him walk off in his own direction. This is not to say he never challenged or became angry with those who make a mockery of his Father's Word (such as the Pharisees or the money-changers in the Temple). But still his mission was to fearlessly proclaim the truth, not impose it at sword's point.

At the Last Supper, Jesus set an example he intended for all Christians, but perhaps especially for those who would exercise some authority in his Church. Washing the feet of his apostles, he came to each of them as a servant. " 'Do you understand,' he said, 'what I have done to you? You call me Master and Lord, and rightly; so I am. If I, then, the Lord and Master, have washed your feet, you should wash each other's feet. I have given you an example so that you may copy what I have done to you. I tell you most solemnly, no servant is greater than his master, no messenger is greater than the man who sent him' " (John 13: 12-16).

A dispute once arose among the apostles as to whom was the greatest. Jesus' response was: "The greatest among you must behave as if he were the youngest, the leader as if he were the one who serves. For who is the greater: the one at the table or the one who serves? The one at table, surely? Yet here am I among you as one who serves!" (Luke 22: 26-27)

7

Service, then, is to be the watchword for those who would exercise authority in Jesus' name. In *The Church Under Tension*, Franciscans Alcuin Coyle and Dismas Bonner tell us that "Jesus made authority in his Church a function of love" and that law and authority must be geared toward service to the Christian community. When law sets up guidelines which are helpful to our growth as Christians, which lead us ever closer to Christ, then it is fulfilling its true purpose. As Fathers Coyle and Bonner point out, "Law either contributes to the orientation of the Christian life or it is useless."

Jesus Rules by Witness, Not Force

He refused to be a political Messiah, ruling by force; he preferred to call himself the Son of Man, who came 'to serve and to give his life as a ransom for many" (Mark 10:45). . . .He bore witness to the truth, but he refused to impose the truth by force on those who spoke against it. . . .From the very origins of the Church the disciples of Christ strove to convert men to faith in Christ as the Lord—not, however, by the use of coercion or by devices unworthy of the Gospel, but by the power, above all, of the Word of God (*Declaration on Religious Freedom*, #11).

Jesus always approached law from this positive point of view. He states that there are two great commandments, summarized briefly: "Love God, and love your neighbor." In the story of the Good Samaritan, he demonstrates what that positive obligation might entail. Repeatedly, he is in conflict with the Pharisees for curing on the Sabbath. Here he shows how the law of love must be the supreme guiding principle in our lives. We must live by the *spirit* of this law and use it to decide how we will act in a specific situation, even if at times it appears to be in conflict with the *letter* of the law.

8

It is possible, Coyle and Bonner continue, that relying too heavily on rules and regulations can really hamper the free and genuine response of the Christian people. For instance, "too much attention to laws regulating prayer, worship and the practice of penance led many Catholics to be quite oblivious of their need for interior prayer, a true spirit of worship, and conversion of heart." It is just too easy to let legalities distract us from the important ideas behind them.

Growth Brings Growing Pains

The maturing Christian community understands authority to be an important guiding principle in its conscience decisions. In fact, the responsible Christian looks eagerly to the teaching of the Church and its bishops in matters of faith and morals, knowing that he or she should be ready, as Vatican II states, "to accept their teaching and adhere to it with religious assent" *(Dogmatic Constitution on the Church,* #25). And they know that this assent should be shown "in a special way to the authentic teaching authority of the Roman Pontiff, even when he is not speaking ex cathedra."

Responsible Christians therefore recognize the value of the Church's authority because when properly exercised as an expression of the Spirit alive in the community it serves, it is one of the brightest lights in the life of a Christian. But as mature Christians, we no longer expect to have our hands held or be given detailed directions for everything we must do. We know we must work that out for ourselves.

Is the Church Getting Harder?

This doesn't make life any easier. There was a lot of security in having everything spelled out for us quite explicitly in our moral and religious lives. We are much like the adolescent who longs for more freedom and then discovers that the responsibility that goes along with it can be a difficult and frightening prospect. But if the authority of the Church is to fulfill its call to service of the Christian community, then like a loving parent it must encourage us to assume this responsi-

9

bility so that we can become free and mature Christians.

Is the Church going soft? If we understand recent changes in the Church as part of our growth toward Christian maturity, then it certainly doesn't seem that way. Growth is always a risk, as it always involves letting go of the things we were once secure in. "The Spirit guarantees continued growth but the Church must take the risk of changing itself if it is to find the fullness of its adult presence in the world," states Father Kennedy. The Church must be constantly ready to deepen its self-understanding and move ahead toward the Kingdom to which it is called.

Greater personal responsibility may indeed seem a bit frightening and risky. But it's not as if we are left entirely alone. After all, the idea of a loving Christian community—which the Church is called to be—is that we can find help, guidance, respect and support from our brothers and sisters, especially those who lead and teach the community. Therefore, at the same time the Church tells us not to shrink from the call to greater maturity, it offers us guidance and direction—ideally in a spirit of service and love.

We also have the promise of Jesus that he is always with us, and with his Church, and that the gates of hell shall not prevail against it.

Questions for Discussion

1. How does the author contrast the "religion of childhood" with "mature religion"?

2. What does theologian John Giles Milhaven mean by "sharing God's dominion"?

3. Why should the *spirit* of the law, rather than the *letter* of the law, guide our lives?

4. How do the two great commandments—love God and love your neighbor—summarize Jesus' approach to law and authority?

5. Do you agree with Father Eugene Kennedy's proposal that the Catholic Christian community is growing more mature in its relationship to God? Why or why not?

Examining Your Conscience Today

by George Alliger and Jack Wintz, O.F.M.

No, the examination of conscience has *not* gone the way of the Latin Mass and the midnight fast before Communion. The Church still considers self-examination relevant for our day, even though our understanding of the practice is developing.

Glancing at the prevailing moods in the Church, we see two different attitudes toward the examination of conscience.

Some people regret that this practice (as they once knew it) has gone out of style in recent years. They long for the time when the Church wasn't so "lax"—when churchgoers reviewed their sins more often and checked their lives more seriously against the Ten Commandments. For them less emphasis on the examination of conscience, like less frequent confessions,

is another sure sign that the moral fiber of the Church is
weakening.

Others feel that the diminished attention given to self-examination is not all bad. "We examined our consciences no end
before Vatican II," they say. "Now we can concentrate on
our positive tasks as Christians, not just our faults." For these
people, the examination of conscience stirs up bad memories:
childhood fears of mortal sin lurking in every corner, frightening times in the confessional with a harsh priest, or distorted
presentations of religion as devoid of warmth and mercy but
obsessed with sin and guilt.

The first group may be consoled to know that the Church
still holds the examination of conscience as vital for all Catholics. Pope Paul insists that it is "a spiritual and ascetic practice
of supreme importance." Church teaching heartily supports
the many Catholics who examine their deeds and attitudes
every evening before bed or at other regular intervals. And at
the beginning of every Mass the Church invites us to examine
our consciences with the words, "Let us call to mind our sins."

The second group can find comfort in the changing attitudes
toward the examination of conscience. Now this exercise fits
more clearly into a framework of the good news of God's love
and forgiveness. Internal attitudes are considered as well as
external acts. And the preoccupation with *individual* evil is
balanced by a better understanding of *social* evil.

Let's Get to the Basics

Before going further, however, let's try to clarify the meaning
of conscience itself. Just what is conscience?

Though conscience is not precisely a feeling, it is closely
associated with our feelings. In fact one way we know our
conscience exists is by the *pain* it sometimes causes us.
"Why do I always *feel* so *guilty*?" cries the anguished heroine
in Ingmar Bergman's film *Face to Face*. We have all felt the
pangs of a "guilty conscience."

14

And yet conscience is much more than a feeling. It is a *power of judgment*. My conscience is my way of judging or discerning whether or not the general contours of my life are in harmony with God's will and whether or not certain actions, omissions or attitudes of mine clash with moral principle.

Sometimes the judgments of conscience are as clear as a bell. I shoplifted this transistor radio and my conscience declares me "guilty" because my action violates a moral law that says stealing is wrong. Sometimes a judgment is difficult to make. After yelling at my child, I wonder, "I *think* she deserved a rebuke and that my anger was constructive—but I'm not *sure*."

Since the operation of conscience or our "moral sense" involves our feelings, it often happens that we wrongly confuse a *feeling* of guilt with a guilty *conscience*. A mother and father discover that their baby has suffocated in its own bed clothings—a terrible tragedy but a complete accident. In their minds the parents know and judge that they were not negligent and so are not responsible for the child's death, yet feelings of guilt may plague them for years. Call this anxiety, insecurity, obsession with guilt, but it is not really a guilty conscience.

A further complication is that although our conscience is a judgment and not a feeling alone, it operates almost instinctively. Pope Paul describes the "moral sense" as "an immediate, we might almost say instinctive, judgment (so primitive is it in our rational process) on the goodness, or the badness of an action." Our conscience is something built deeply into our personality and it learns to function almost automatically.

Why *Examine* Conscience?

We do not examine our conscience to become scrupulous or fearful. Our conscience is not meant to be an enemy but a friendly guide to our fulfillment as human beings. We do not review our lives just to feel uncomfortable, but as an aid to our growth as God's sons and daughters. Vatican II in its *Pastoral Constitution on the Church in the Modern World* has described conscience as God's "voice" echoing in the depth of our being and the following of which is "the very dignity of man" (# 16). And we know from the Gospel that God's voice is loving and calls us not to fear or diminishment but to happiness and fullness of life.

The most important reason for examining our conscience is to help us discern whether or not our lives conform to God's best wishes for us—to make sure that our basic direction is God-ward. Our fundamental slant, or decision, in life is either toward God (grace) or away from him (sin). We check on our conscience to assure ourselves that our general direction is the right one and getting better.

Reviewing the "basic slant" of our lives is a central aspect of the examination of conscience. In the past Catholic theology put more emphasis on the external behavior of the individual. Historians say this emphasis originally grew out of the Roman Empire, where law and the legal system were of primary importance. If this is true, we can see how the examination of conscience could become the comparing of ourselves with a list of prohibited things ("you shall not kill, you shall not steal") and the gauging of how we measured up. What seemed important was the code of laws and our corresponding list of transgressions.

Recently the Church has placed more stress on overall patterns and the *inner attitude* of an individual. This emphasis would mean that after an examination of conscience we do not come up merely with a "grocery list" of individual sins so much as an understanding of our attitudes and the basic direction—or drift—of our lives. Am I headed toward God or not? Am I really loving toward others? What are the motives behind my conduct? What dangerous patterns do I see there? The exami-nation of conscience today is looking at the *forest* and not only at the trees.

The stress on attitude is significant, because it would be possi-ble for a person to *do* everything right in a technical sense, obey all the Church laws, and yet have a narrow unchristian attitude towards God, people and life in general. This is what

16

Jesus seems to point out in his parable of the tax-collector and the Pharisee. The Pharisee "did" everything quite right—he fasted, gave to the poor, observed the laws—but his heart was actually proud and selfish. The tax-collectors who admitted his sins, was really more in touch with his conscience, and Jesus commended him and not the Pharisee.

Of course in examining our conscience it is good to pinpoint particular sins. Haziness is not a virtue. But we must also ask the basic questions and, what is more, discern our *good* qualities and *good* deeds so as to thank God and foster further development.

Towards a More Social Conscience

In addition to more stress on the inner attitude of an individual, the Church also has grown increasingly aware of our social responsibilities. More and more we see that sin is not only a private affair but one that concerns my relationship to the larger community—to society both local and global. Vatican II's *Pastoral Constitution on the Church in the Modern World* (# 30) insists that the contemporary Christian cannot rest content "with a merely individualistic morality. It grows increasingly true that the obligations of justice and love are fulfilled only if each person, contributing to the common good, . . .also promotes and assists the public and private institutions dedicated to bettering the conditions of human life." The document criticizes those who like to profess "grand and noble sentiments" but live as if they "cared nothing for the needs of society."

What the Church is telling us today is that it is not enough to examine ourselves merely in terms of personal piety but in terms of our contributions to the good or evil of society. Have we been actively concerned with the elimination of hunger, disease, discrimination, war, poverty, injustice in the total community to which we belong? Do we educate ourselves on these issues? Do we vote responsibly? Our examination of conscience must now include these questions.

Methods for Examination of Conscience

There is more than one way to examine our conscience, of course, but practical guides can be helpful as long as we remember that they are just that—guides—and not the only options.

Examination of conscience is important for all—just as thought and reflection are important for all human beings. This practice is not only for people following a religious vocation. Nor is it meant solely as a preparation for confession. A method like the following can be used by anyone and at anytime and even serve as a helpful aid for private prayer and reflection.

St. Ignatius' Five-Step Plan

Like several other saints, St. Ignatius of Loyola, developed a form—or framework—for the examination of conscience. An adaptation of his five-fold method is presented here:
1. Turn consciously to God and *thank* him for all his gifts. Gratitude is the natural response to grace enriching our lives.
2. Ask God to help you *be honest* in looking at yourself.
3. *Review* your actions and attitudes starting from the last time you examined your conscience.
4. *Ask God's pardon* for faulty responses to his grace.
5. *Resolve* to respond more fully to his grace.

This method needn't take long. And it is not necessary to give more attention to the review-your-actions section than to the others, especially if it leads to scrupulosity or unhealthy introspection.

Examination of "Consciousness"

A number of spiritual writers are observing today that the exercise is an examination of *consciousness* rather than of *conscience*. And really it's an examination *by* conscience rather than *of* conscience. For with the aid of conscience— that is, by the gift and power of spiritual judgment or discernment—we explore our consciousness: the whole state of our conscious experience. We try to discern within ourselves the movement of God (and of evil) and our patterns of response.

A Contemporary Guide for Examining Your Conscience
*In broad outline and spirit this examination follows
the form suggested by the revised Rite of Penance.*

My Relationship to God   *"You shall love the Lord your
God with your whole heart."*

1.   Is my whole life directed toward loving God and seeking his kingdom and plan for humanity? Or are personal greed and the things of this world my basic object of devotion?
2.   Do I accept with my whole heart the revelation of God's love through Jesus and do I respond fully to the call of his Spirit in my life?
3.   Do I pray sufficiently each day and seek to have a continuous spirit of prayer? Do I turn to God in good times and bad and in times of temptation? Do I listen with an open and humble heart and am I ready to accept the inner conversion to which he invites me? Do I praise and thank him for his gifts?
4.   Do I worship God as an active member of the faith community Christ founded, the Church? Am I conscious of and responsive to the Body of Christ, local and universal? Do I participate fully in the Mass each Sunday and in the whole sacramental life of the Church? Do I accept Church teaching and authority in a spirit of faith and cooperation?
5.   Do I take steps to deepen and increase my understanding of the faith? Do I profess and live it courageously?
6.   Have I shown reverence for God in my speech and in my attitude toward religious symbols? Have I elevated things like money, status, superstition or occult practices to the level of false gods?

My Relationship to Others   *"Love one another as I
have loved you."*

1.   Do I truly love my neighbors—as myself? Do I aid or obstruct their progress toward God and fuller life?

Have I used or exploited others for my own selfish interests?

2. Am I caring toward my family? Do I show fidelity, patience, reverence and love to my spouse, children, parents, brothers, sisters? Have I shown good example? Fulfilled my respective role?

3. Do I deal honestly and truthfully with others? Have I harmed anyone by deceit, rash judgment, detraction, calumny or broken agreements? Have I worked honestly, upheld contracts, paid fair wages?

4. Have my relations to others been faithful and chaste? Have I sexually exploited or demeaned another? Am I guilty of such violations of chastity as adultery, fornication, or conversation that is indecent or cheapens human dignity?

5. Have I hated others, shown prejudice or discrimination toward them? Have I stolen or damaged the property of others? Have I returned or paid for stolen or damaged goods? Do I share what God has given me with those in need?

6. Have I injured the life, limb or reputation of others? Have I upheld and protected the right to life at all levels? Have I procured or cooperated in abortion or not revered the human dignity of the aged, the retarded, deformed or mentally ill? Am I violent? Do I strive to reduce violence around me?

7. Do I bring the good news of the gospel to others? Do I promote Christian values and the life of the Church on all levels of human society? Do I work and pray for Christian unity? Do I try to heal the wounds of the Church or do I inflame them? Do I support and involve myself in the Christian community or parish to which I belong?

8. Do I obey legitimate authority? Do I exercise leadership and authority in a spirit of Christian service?

9. Do I work for the betterment of human society? Do I try to be informed and actively concerned about social and political issues that affect the common good whether on the local, national or global level.

10. According to my role in life, do I seek to eliminate

from the world whatever keeps my brothers and sisters from the full human development intended by their creator: poverty, disease, hunger, injustice, discrimination, oppressive laws and structures, unequal distribution of world resources? Am I—is my country—wasteful or using up an unjust amount of the world's resources (food, fuel, minerals, etc.)? Do I support according to my means and abilities, organizations which work for social improvement?

My Personal Growth in Christ
"Be perfect as your Father is perfect."

1. Is Christ and his way of living the basic goal of my life? What inclinations and attitudes within me are hindrances to my growth and development as God's son or daughter? Am I too self-centered? Do I work on controlling dangerous attitudes like pride, arrogance, jealousy, avarice, lust, intemperance, self-sufficiency, prejudice? Do I explore my motives and overall pattern of conduct? Do I make full use of my talents and gifts?

2. Do I try to keep a cheerful, positive disposition? Do I give into depression and self-pity? Do I put myself down? Do I let unfounded fears limit my potential and personal freedom? Have I let fear prevent me from following my conscience? Do I seek counseling, spiritual direction and other aids to personal growth, when needed? Do I take care of my health? Overeat, over-drink, take harmful drugs?

3. Do I have a wholesome attitude toward my own sexuality? Have I wilfully indulged in thoughts, actions, reading, entertainment that are contrary to the dignity and proper meaning of sex?

4. Do I take time for my spiritual growth? Do I have a wholesome spirit of penance and self-denial as taught by Jesus? Do I observe the days of penance established by the Church? Is personal renewal and on-going inner conversion a priority in my life? Am I open to change and the call to fuller life prompted by God's Spirit in my heart?

Questions for Discussion

1. What is *conscience*? How does it operate?

2. Why should we examine our conscience?

3. Why is the *inner attitude* of the individual important in the examination of conscience?

4. Why must our examination of conscience be made in terms of our contributions to the good and evil of society, as well as in terms of personal piety?

5. Explain St. Ignatius' "Five-Step Plan" for examining conscience. What method do you use?

How to Go to Confession Using the New Ritual

by Leonard Foley, O.F.M.

The first question many people ask when they hear there is a new ritual for confession is "Now can we all get general absolution, so we don't have to go into the box?" Or the questioner is at the other extreme and says anxiously: "You mean I have to get up in public and confess my sins?"

The new ritual's answer to both these questions is no. It states: "Individual, integral confession and absolution remain the only ordinary way for the faithful to reconcile themselves to God and the Church, unless physical or moral necessity excuses." The ritual then describes this necessity as "grave need, namely when, in view of the number of penitents, sufficient confessors are not available to hear individual confessions properly within a suitable period of time, so that the penitents would, through

25

no fault of their own, have to go without sacramental grace or Holy Communion for a long time." As for privacy, it is still the same. The penitent confesses individually to the priest, either in the confessional or face to face.

New Understanding Needed

But these are not the basic questions. For one reason and another, many Catholics don't celebrate the sacrament at all any more. Others feel it is a sort of dusting-off-the-angels luxury for holy types. Still other Catholics now ask, as Protestants once did, "Why do I have to confess to another human being?"

It should be said right now that the new ritual, *as ritual,* is not going to answer these problems. Unless there is a thorough re-understanding of sin, God's redeeming work in Christ, reconciliation, Church and sacrament, it is to be feared that the new ritual will fail in its purpose.

In fact, many will probably be disappointed in the new ritual as such. There is not that much difference in the actual external ceremonies and words compared to the old form. If you want to be downright legalistic about it, all the penitent really says in the new rite (besides the confession of sin) is: an Act of Contrition, the Sign of the Cross, Amen (twice) and a response. "His mercy endures forever."

The Spirit and Meaning of the New Rite

Evidently the bishops must have something deeper in mind. The most important part of knowing "How to confess," therefore, is the capturing of the new outlook behind the revised ritual. If you don't mind, then, I'd like to postpone a discussion of the actual ritual and begin with what I will call the spirit breathing forth from the pages of the fairly large ritual volume published in Rome.

Leaders of the Church are telling us that whether for mortal or venial sinfulness this sacrament is a very special and important celebration. It is not something to be taken lightly or routinely, or done merely to make someone "feel better" or to unload a burden of sin in an action that has no relationship with the rest of our lives. In other words, we are being asked to celebrate the sacrament seriously or, in my opinion, not at all.

There are several new emphases in the ritual; none of them is new, though some have perhaps been overshadowed in recent centuries.

A Warm, Forgiving God

Among the essentials of the sacrament, the most obvious should be: God is a warm, loving, forgiving God. The primary fact about the sacrament of confession is that God loves us so much that like "The Hound of Heaven" in Francis Thompson's famous poem he will never stop pursuing us so that he may heal our agony and our aloneness. If we do not have the fundamental realization that we are approaching a merciful God, a passionately loving God, then the sacrament can become merely an ordeal—something you go through, so that you come with a ticket that says that God has nothing on you.

This is not the thrust of the ritual at all. The overall, the overwhelming truth about the sacrament of reconciliation is that God wants to heal us more than we want to be healed. But this God must be seen in his warmth, and therefore we always must come back to the glorious fact of the Incarnation of the Second Person of the Trinity. God wanted to speak to us in our language, to touch us with flesh like our own, to look into our eyes with human eyes and to speak to us with human words. And so we have Jesus, the sign that is the Sacrament of the loving God.

If anyone wanted to know how good God was, all he needed to do was to look at Jesus, listen to him and receive his healing. It is the same today. We need to realize that this same divine and human Jesus is eagerly and ardently welcoming us to reconciliation and healing and peace. He is not interested in punishment and bawlings out. We must first experience his love, and it will prompt us to take care of whatever reparation and reform is needed.

Church Must Be Warm

How do we see with our own eyes and hear with our own ears the human-divine warmth of Jesus' love? We see and hear and touch him in that group of people whom he has left behind to be precisely his visible presence, that group of people whom we call the Church. The Church is called to be the convincing sign of God's healing. To the degree that the Church—and that means the local parish—is not a welcoming, forgiving, open, reconciling, Christlike community, to that degree they—we—are obstructing the continuing work of Christ on earth today.

The seven individual sacraments are going to be greatly handicapped, (God's work in them, that is) if the sacrament *of the Church* is not first of all a convincing sign of the never-ending forgiveness and love of the Father and of Jesus and the Spirit. It is the *community* that is involved in reconciliation. The community welcomes all sinners. And so any reform and revision of the ritual of confession must be accompanied by the never-ending reform and purification and Christianization of the community in which all of us sinners live.

Of course, the warmth and the love of the Church must be seen in one particular person, the priest. The community may be warm, but if the priest himself in his celebration of the sacrament does not personally represent, in a convincing way, the love and mercy of Christ, then again the redeeming work of Christ is obstructed.

Yes it is true, as we have always said, the sacrament is valid; that is, something happens even if the priest is unworthy. But not everything happens that God wants to happen unless the priest is the warm, welcoming, kind, patient, understanding Christ.

The new ritual therefore mentions at the very beginning that the priest should *welcome* the penitent and speak to him or her kindly. This is not to say priests have never done this. It is, however, to emphasize that this is the atmosphere in which God's grace works best.

A Deeper Look at Sin

A second consideration in studying the new ritual is a deepened understanding of the meaning of sin. Modern theologians have pointed out what mankind has known from the beginning: that sin is not only individual external actions. These particular actions, like unkind words or the hand stealing from the cash register or the arm striking another person, are only the tips of the iceberg. Sinfulness lies deep in our persons. It is not something that we turn on and off like an electric switch. What somebody does at 12:05 represents the attitude he had at noon and 11:30 and 11, and the attitude that he still has at 1 and 2 and 3 o'clock unless he makes a definite effort to change the spirit which is filling his life.

People are sometimes puzzled by this explanation, because one conclusion from it is that a person never really knows when someone *begins* to commit sin or *how far* along the way he or she is. Someone may be developing a sinful attitude which, if allowed to continue will become so serious as to break his relationship with God. But how far he has gone along that line, I don't know.

And so in answering the questions of worried parents, the priest may say, "I don't know whether it is a mortal sin for Johnny to miss Mass on Sunday." And the parents reply is: "Well, if *you* don't know, then who does?" And next comes: "It seems that nothing is a sin anymore!"

Sin Is an Attitude, a Spirit

No one is saying that. They are merely saying that sin is a far more pervasive thing than the single, countable, external action that we can see. Sin is a spirit just as faith and love and hope are a spirit. They all go on in a man or woman's heart. They are not, as I have said, turned on and off like electric current.

Sin is the willingness to let my relationship with God be strained, or when the strain goes on long enough, to be broken.

29

That is what we mean by mortal sinfulness: the breaking of a relationship with God. This happens in a person's heart long before it appears in his or her bodily actions.

From "Grocery List" to a Searching of Hearts

What has this to do with the sacrament of reconciliation? First of all, it would seem that we must get away from the "grocery list"—a numerical recitation of things that were perhaps sinful but often were not: "I forgot my morning prayers; I forgot my evening prayers" (To *forget* anything cannot be a sin), "I ate meat on Friday, I thought it was Thursday." (One can never mistakenly commit a sin.) Things like that represent too great a concern with a certain external respectability without an equal concern for the *spirit* which underlies my whole life.

Of course, many of the people who made these "nice" confessions were good people. But even the best people in the world have at least what might be called a minor infection, a certain spirit of venial sinfulness: selfishness, neglect, petty pride, etc. What we need to do is to look into our hearts and see the set of *motives* which prompt almost everything in our lives.

Searching Out the Real Evil

For example, there are people who by temperament are very efficient in running things. That talent can become their sinfulness if they become domineering and have no respect for other people's wishes or feelings or rights. And this one single fact can be the tragedy in their lives and others'. And all the while they may have been confessing that they have forgotten their morning prayers, or they came late for Mass because they had a flat tire. They are totally oblivious to the *real* evil in their lives.

To celebrate the sacrament, then, is first of all to recognize the evil that is in me, to admit it, to separate from it all that is not my fault, all that is mere temptation or emotion, and then to look at my real sinfulness there before me and realize that it is evil, that it is straining—if it has not broken—my relationship to God. Only if I am a sinner do I have any reason to celebrate the sacrament of reconciliation.

Sin Is Social

The third great emphasis at least implicit in the new ritual is the socialness of sin. Evil gets hardened in the structures of society, of family life, of individual life. The world is blotched with the results of some people's sin, making or leaving other people ignorant, poor, deprived of elementary rights, starving physically, emotionally and intellectually. Marriage and family life can settle into routine coldness, breaks in communication, isolation—to the lifelong damage of both spouses and children.

Some sins are evidently social—striking someone in the face, taking his money, ruining his reputation, spreading disease of mind or body. But the deepest reason why sin is social lies in the very way God made us. We are meant to form a loving community, one in which members help (not hinder) each other to reach full development as human beings and as God's family.

Reconciliation Is Central

And that leads us to the central word which the Church is emphasizing in the new ritual: *reconciliation.* When I allow sin to possess my spirit, I become a stranger to myself and to my neighbor and to my God. I no longer sit in the circle of the family. I am the son who has left the father and gone off to seek his own selfish pleasure. *I need reconciliation, forgiveness.* Reconciliation is putting back together what once was one. It is rediscovering unity. It is showing that there is a fundamental agreement between two people who once seemed incompatible. God always wants reconciliation—things to be right again between us. Human nature always *needs* reconciliation, because we cannot be "right" with God if we are not right with our neighbor.

We see here the simple unity of the commandments: Love

31

God-neighbor-self. You can't do one without the other. And if you are unreconciled to one, you are unreconciled to the other.

Jesus formed a reconciled and reconciling Church, his Body, the sign of his forgiveness. If I am a member who has experienced the warmth of this community, I will have no question as to why I can be, or should be, reconciled to God through this sign of Christ. If I do not see this community as the visible expression of Christ today, then all the arguments in the world will not "prove" why I should not simply "go straight to God" for forgiveness.

Using the New Ritual

Only if all these elements are present—a realization of the love and mercy of God, a welcoming community, a kindly and understanding priest, my awareness of responsibility for others in my sinfulness—only then will there be flesh and blood on the meager bones of the new ritual. The "bones" of the three modes of celebrating the sacrament are these: The first is the reconciliation of *individual penitents*, that is one priest, one penitent; the second is what we have learned to call the *communal celebration* of the sacrament in which a group of people gather together for prayers and hymns and examination of conscience; then each goes privately and individually to the confessional; and the third is what we have always described as *emergency general absolution*.

Because you as an individual may soon have the opportunity to use the new ritual at your parish, it will be good to look at the rite of *the reconciliation of individual penitents* more in detail. First, there is an *option* of using the traditional confessional or coming face to face with the priest. The ritual asks the priest and penitent to prepare by prayer. Right here we have the key to a fruitful celebration of the sacrament. Imagine the difference it will make if the priest and the penitent, kneeling together in church, perhaps aloud, but at least silently, pray for light, for strength, for healing. The whole atmosphere of the sacrament is then charged with the presence of God.

Words of Welcome and Encouragement by Priest

Next, the priest welcomes the penitent kindly and makes the atmosphere such that the penitent is fully aware that this is the divine welcome of the mercy of God. The penitent then says one of the few things the ritual instructs him or her to say: "In the name of the Father, and of the Son, and of the Holy Spirit."

Again the priest urges the penitent to have confidence. The confessor may do this in a variety of ways. And this, incidentally, is one of the features of the new ritual. In many of the elements of the sacrament the ritual gives five, six or seven alternatives. This is so the sacrament does not become a hardened ritual.

Recently Father Gerald Broccolo of the Archdiocesan Liturgical Commission of Chicago wrote a letter to the bishops complaining about the little leaflets that he anticipates will be coming out telling people how to go to confession—as if there is *one single way.*

Actually there are many alternatives. For instance, as I said, the priest at this point may speak words of encouragement in many different ways.

Scriptural Reading

Next there is the reading of the word of God. This is one of the emphases of the new ritual. Some selection of the Bible chosen by the penitent or the priest is now read (or it may be read as part of the preparation for the sacrament). Now again if we realize that the Bible is the living, personal, here-and-now voice of God calling us to conversion and to his grace, then this can be a very dramatic and powerful help to contrition and conversion. The reading of the word of God again permits of almost limitless alternatives. The priest or penitent may say a portion of Scripture from memory or may read it. According to circumstances, this may be short or long.

Confession, Penance, Absolution

Then the penitent confesses his or her sins in whatever way seems best. There is nothing new here.

The priest then is called upon to help the penitent make a complete confession if necessary, encourage him or her to true sorrow, give suitable counsel, instruct the penitent if necessary, etc. The priest then imposes a penance, which "may suitably take the form of prayer, self-denial, and especially service of one's neighbor and works of mercy. These will underscore the social aspect of sin and its forgiveness.

Next the penitent expresses his or her sorrow for sin. This may be done in the traditional Act of Contrition or in the penitent's own words.

The priest imparts absolution while extending his hand(s) over the penitent. The new formula stresses that reconciliation comes from the Father, shows the connection between the reconciliation of the sinner and the death and resurrection of Christ, and stresses the role of the Holy Spirit in forgiveness. It also underlines the fact that reconciliation with God is asked for and given through the ministry of the Church. The penitent answers, "Amen."

The sacrament concludes quickly with a "proclamation of praise" of the mercy of God. The priest says "Give thanks to the Lord, for he is good," and the penitent responds, "His mercy endures forever." The priest then dismisses the penitent in these or similar words: "The Lord has freed you from your sins. Go in peace."

And So. . .

Using the new ritual means more than memorizing a few new phrases. We are being called to a deepening of our whole Christian life, particularly its aspects of genuine repentance, a sense of the reconciling Christian community, and the ongoing, lifelong process of conversion. Above all, we are called to believe that we really have something to *celebrate*—namely, a visible sign of the reconciliation only God can give, and which he generously offers.

'

Questions for Discussion

1. What does the author say is the overwhelming thrust of the confession ritual?

2. How does the author explain the meaning of sin?

3. How can we avoid a "grocery list" attitude toward confession?

4. The Church emphasizes the word *reconciliation* in the new confession ritual. What does it mean in terms of the commandments? of the community?

5. What are the three modes of celebrating the sacrament?

6. Describe the "reconciliation of individual penitents" in detail.

Confessing Face-to-Face

by Leonard Foley, O.F.M.

photos by Anne Bingham

Most Catholics are anxious about what they are expected to say and do in the new confession rite. Must they learn a whole new way of going to confession to replace what they've been doing all their lives? Not really.

What is *new* in the new rite is an increased seriousness, a broader view of conversion as an ongoing process, an insistence on the presence of God and of the Christian community, a greater realization of the social nature of sin. It is hoped that the new ritual will make the sacrament a more prayerful celebration of God's mercy and healing power, and bring us to a greater awareness of the dying and rising with Christ which is the Christian's never-ending task and privilege.

Using the confessional "box" is still everyone's right. But the *option* of face-to-face confession is intended to effect a more personal and realistic experience for both penitent and confessor. This atmosphere is conducive to a more "in depth" consideration of the direction of one's whole life, the deeper roots of sin, the concrete circumstances of life to which the gospel must be applied.

The greater responsibility for the fruitful use of face-to-face confession lies with the priest. He will have to be a warm and kindly "welcomer," willing to accept both the pain and the spiritual yearning of the person before him. And he will have to be able to combine a sense of the solemnity of a sacramental action with the down-to-earth understanding of the penitent's experience in the "real world."

To be specific, there is really only one new aspect of the sacrament as far as the penitent is concerned: the expression of sorrow (act of contrition) is now a distinct act rather than something done while the priest is giving absolution. Also, the penitent is asked to say "Amen" to the absolution and to give a brief response ("His mercy endures forever") to the priest's final proclamation of praise of God at the dismissal ("Give thanks to the Lord, for he is good").

There should be no real concern about what to do. Cards will be available to help the penitent express sorrow (10 different forms). The penitent should simply meet the priest and let the encounter develop as seems fitting.

The following is an imaginary face-to-face confession. It is not the shortest form possible, nor does it go into the detail of what might easily be a long discussion of the penitent's spiritual life. It is meant to represent an ordinary celebration of the sacrament.

Preparation

The "success" of the sacrament will be determined by the seriousness with which we approach it. The ritual suggests that both priest and penitent prepare themselves by prayer: the priest to receive enlightenment and charity from the Holy Spirit; the penitent to place his or her life next to the example and commandments of Christ and to pray for forgiveness. Perhaps the most effective beginning is silent or spontaneous prayer by priest and penitent together.

Welcome

Priest: Good afternoon. I'm glad to meet you.

Penitent: Good afternoon, Father. I'm a little nervous about this, since I've never gone to confession this way before.

Priest: There's no need to worry. We'll just follow a simple routine. The main thing we want to remember is that we're in God's presence and that this is a special time of forgiveness and grace. Let's begin, then, by making the Sign of the Cross together and taking the words very seriously.

Priest and Penitent (slowly): In the name of the Father, and of the Son, and of the Holy Spirit. Amen.

Prayer

Priest: I'd like to pray now that we may both be open to what God is offering us in this sacrament. If you wish to pray in your own words too, fine. Otherwise we'll just pray in silence for a little while.

Priest: Loving Father, you are with us. We trust in your graciousness and mercy and we beg you to open our minds and hearts to your truth and love. Give us both the grace to be humble and honest, to face the reality of sin and also the mystery of your infinite love.
Perhaps, after a few moments of silence, the penitent may be moved to say something like:

Penitent: Dear Lord, help me to make a good confession, to be truly sorry, and to be willing to let you change my life.

Hearing God's Word

Priest: In this new rite the Church asks us to listen first to the word of God. It is God who brings you here, and calls you personally to deepen your conversion from sin and your turning to him. So we listen now to God speaking personally and seriously to us.
There are dozens of options as to what Scripture may be read— very brief or long passages. Either penitent or priest may do the reading. One example is Luke 15, 1-7.

Priest or Penitent: "The tax collectors and sinners were all gathering around to hear him, at which the Pharisees and the scribes murmured, 'This man welcomes sinners and eats with

them.' Then he addressed this parable to them: 'Who among you, if he has 100 sheep and loses one of them, does not leave the 99 in the wasteland and follow the lost one until he finds it? And when he finds it, he puts it on his shoulders in jubilation. Once arrived home, he invites friends and neighbors in and says to them, "Rejoice with me because I have found my lost sheep." I tell you, there will likewise be more joy in heaven over one repentant sinner than over 99 righteous people who have no need to repent.' "

Priest: Let's just think about this call of God to us for a few minutes.
Silence. Or, possibly, some spontaneous prayer by priest and/or penitent.

41

Confession of Sin

Penitent: Father, it's been about three months since my last confession. I am married and have three children. I guess my worst sin is the way I treat my husband and children. We have a fairly good relationship, but I do let myself get into moods when I just withdraw into myself. I resent the work I have to do. I feel my husband could do more and the kids could be less demanding. So sometimes I feel sorry for myself, and let things slide.

Priest: It's good that you are able to admit this.

Penitent: I realize that it's more than half my fault, and I want to do something about it.

Priest: It affects your whole life when you let yourself feel this way?

Penitent: Yes, I don't pray well, or really love my husband as I want to, or my children.

42

Priest: Is this a long-standing fault?

Penitent: I'm beginning to see that I had something of this before I was married, when I was at home. I tended to pout when things didn't go right, and to sort of wallow in self-pity.

Priest: What do you think is at the bottom of it?

Penitent: I really don't know. In general I have a fairly happy life, except for this attitude that I nourish and really don't do much about. I'm sorry for what it does to me and to my husband and children. I know God is calling me to rise above it.

Priest: The best thing I can tell you, on a human level, is to keep trying to discover what lies beneath this sinfulness. Maybe you're too insecure, or you need more than normal encouragement. Maybe you're too sensitive, or want too much attention. Don't analyze yourself to death, but look beneath the surface and try gradually to know yourself better.

But the main thing we have to remember is that God is calling you to be more completely possessed by the Spirit. Any sin, all sinfulness spoils God's plan for us. It takes something away from our love of God and others. It makes us less able to do the one thing we are called to do—be perfectly open to God's coming, completely possessed by the Spirit.

Now, as a penance, is there any one thing you feel would be helpful in overcoming this attitude?

Penitent: I really couldn't say, Father. I know it's a long process.

Priest: Well, suppose that every morning this week you get down on your knees and, whatever other prayers you say, you look ahead to something that's liable to happen to you that day. Ask the Father to help you at that moment, to fill you with his strength—so that you can reject being resentful and over-sorry for yourself. O.K.?

Penitent: Fine, Father, I'll do that.

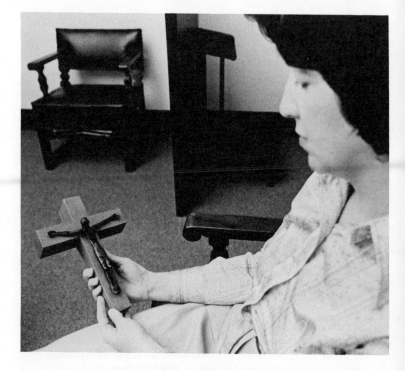

Expression of Sorrow

Priest: Now, in a special way, as an outward sign of your desire to be forgiven and healed by God, please express your sorrow for your sinfulness.
The penitent may say the familiar Act of Contrition, or use one of the several prayers on the card, or use his or her own words.

Penitent: God our Father, I thank you for letting me see my sinfulness and giving me the power to admit it. I put myself into your hands. I am sorry for the harm I have done to your love within me and for spoiling my love for my husband and my children. I know what you are calling me to. I am determined to let your Spirit possess my mind and my heart and my weakness, so that I can follow Jesus as you want me to. Amen.

Absolution

Priest: God blesses you for what he has been able to do in you. And now, through Jesus, through the Body of Jesus which I have been called to represent visibly to you, God gives you the infallible sign of his forgiveness.
The priest extends his hands over the penitent's head.

Priest: God, the Father of mercies,
through the death and resurrection of his Son
has reconciled the world to himself
and sent the Holy Spirit among us
for the forgiveness of sins;
through the ministry of the Church
may God give you pardon and peace,
and I absolve you from your sins
in the name of the Father, and of the Son,
and of the Holy Spirit.

Penitent: Amen.

Proclamation of Praise of God

Priest: God has blessed you. Now show your gratitude for his mercy by a prayer of thanks and praise. Please answer "Your mercy is forever" to each of the short prayers I say:

Priest: God our Father, we give you our hearts.

Penitent: Your mercy is forever.

Priest: Son of God, Jesus our Brother, we praise your name.

Penitent: Your mercy is forever.

Priest: Spirit of God, possess us with your power.

Penitent: Your mercy is forever.

Priest: The Lord has freed you from your sins. Go in peace.

Penitent: Thank you, Father. This has been very good for me. I think I see a little better what it's all about. I'll see you again. Goodbye.

Priest: Goodbye. God bless you.

Every confession is unique, because each life is unique. The above "sample" is an attempt to show how penitent and priest relate to each other in view of the particular problems, faith, attitude and circumstances of the penitent. Much will depend on the charity, understanding and creativity of the priest. But the penitent must bring to the situation a certain willingness to go beneath the surface and to be led to change and growth—the ongoing, never-finished conversion to Christ.

Understanding Changes in the Mass —Ten Familiar Gripes Answered

by Jack Wintz, O.F.M.

People don't gripe about the essential meaning of the Eucharist. For instance, you don't hear Catholics mutter: "I can't stand the Mass as a sign of Christ's saving presence among us or of the unity of Christians." You never hear Uncle Ben explode: "I'm really frosted by the central gesture of the Eucharist—Christ handing over his body to his Father and to us and inviting our imitation."

No, Catholics revere the Eucharist as the central focus of their lives. This was demonstrated by the thousands of Catholics who streamed to Philadelphia for the International Eucharistic Congress in 1976. But their attitude toward *the way the ritual of the Mass has been carried out* since Vatican II is not always without some apprehension, misunderstanding and, yes, even gripes. These complaints often stem from the fear that past values have been downgraded or threatened by the change which has affected our familiar patterns of worship.

The following *10 gripes about the Mass* point up 10 areas of possible confusion and frustration. Perhaps the explanations set forth in this chapter can help clear up some of the misunderstanding.

   The Solemnity Is Gone!

The Mass used to be reverent and dignified. Now it's often a "hippie jamboree" with guitars, folk songs and secular music. Some people don't even genuflect anymore.

Until Vatican II, Catholic liturgy was pretty well identified with the Latin liturgy, with solemn Gregorian chant, with

majestic bows and clouds of rising incense. Catholic solemnity was unsurpassable and it mirrored perfectly our views of God as the eternal majestic Lord serenely enthroned beyond the changing winds of history.

But history shows that prayer styles change. David leapt and danced before the ark. The psalmist praised God with the "rippling of the harp" and with the "music of zither and lyre." The early Christians sometimes bubbled over into tongues of praise, and at times St. Paul had to complain that the distinction between the Mass and a drinking party was getting fuzzy. So we shouldn't feel we have to lock our Church into one style of worship or one that makes solemnity the only priority.

Certain insights of Vatican II have allowed us to see God not only in some far off, silent and eternal sphere but also as very much alive in our history and in the pulsebeat of our time. This realization of the God *within* our changing times (as well as beyond it) has led some people to feel comfortable with new forms of worship which include folk music, banners, films and news headlines.

Many complain that the dignity and solemnity and prayerful atmosphere that surrounded the Latin liturgy have been bull-dozed out of the Mass too hastily, and maybe they are right in a good many instances. That the Church recognizes a variety of prayer styles is demonstrated today in a typical parish where you can attend a quiet Mass without singing, a guitar or folk Mass, a Mass sung in English with organ, and perhaps somewhere in the city, depending on diocesan regulations, even an all Latin Mass.

 There's Too Much Noise!

The atmosphere used to be silent and prayerful. Private thanks-giving after communion used to be so special.

Maybe the noise level in some Masses after Vatican II did get a little out of hand—especially if no time at all was allotted to quiet reflection. Although the Church definitely encourages active participation, it has also clearly stated, in the *General Instruction* of the new Roman Missal, "Silence at designated times is also part of the celebration."

Pastor and writer, Father Joseph Champlin, sees the Church as coming back to a better balance between silence and participa-tion. "We have, over the last decade, come full circle," he writes in *The Mass in a World of Change*. "Silent Masses with mute spectators in the pews was the pattern not so long ago. Then the push for participation led us to stress singing and speaking as the proper activity for people during liturgical worship. Silence seemed out of place, something wrong for parishes truly concerned about active involvement of the faithful in the sacred mysteries. Now, however, a balance urged at Vatican II and confirmed in the reformed missal is the sought-after goal."

Regarding silent prayer after communion, actually the Church still considers it important. In fact, the new Roman Missal frankly expects the individual Catholic to be recollected after receiving the Lord. "After communion," directs the new missal, "he praises God in his heart."

Perhaps, as Father Champlin suggests, "Silent Masses are 'out'; yet silence within Mass is 'in.' "

 Those Lay Lectors and Distributors!

Why do we train and ordain priests and anoint their hands, if we're going to give their sacred duties to the laity? The Mass is something sacred.

This complaint suffers from a devalued notion of the laity and of Baptism. The honor and value that Baptism places on a human being is actually more striking, comparatively speaking, than the honor that ordination adds to the already baptized Christian. As Jesuit author Daniel O'Hanlon writes, "to value ordination above Baptism would be to make a serious mistake."

A healthy respect for the priest, who alone is designated to preside over the Mass and make Christ's Body and Blood present, does not require us to downgrade the laity. To keep the laity from fuller participation in the Eucharist is to discredit their dignity and to resist the mind of the Church, which "earnestly desires that all the faithful be led to the full, conscious and active participation in liturgical celebrations which is demanded by the very nature of the liturgy. Such participation by the Christian people . . . is their right and duty by reason of their baptism" (*Constitution on The Sacred Liturgy*, No. 14). So declared Vatican II.

The Church encourages pastors to "recognize and promote the dignity as well as the responsibility of the layman in the Church" (*Dogmatic Constitution on the Church*, No. 37) and it implements such exhortations by specific instructions giving the laity more active roles in the Church. Since the early 60's various Church documents have ushered in an era of lay lectors and commentators. In 1969 and in 1973, Pope Paul issued instructions authorizing lay men and lay women as extraordinary ministers of the Eucharist under a variety of circumstances.

Greater lay participation in the Mass does not imply the

slightest lessening of the sacredness of the Mass or of the priesthood. Rather it reflects our increasing awareness of the dignity and sacredness with which God looks upon each of his sons and daughters.

 Women Don't Belong in the Sanctuary!

St. Paul said it so clearly: "Women are to remain quiet at meetings since they have no permission to speak; they must keep in the background. . ." (I Cor. 14, 34).

St. Paul was apparently accommodating himself to the cultural customs of his time and settling a point of order for the Church in Corinth. Paul's approach was to take people *where they were*. For example, slavery was part of the social system of his time, and so Paul realistically offered this advice frequently: slaves, be obedient to your masters. Just as Christ's teaching about the dignity and equality of human beings gradually led to the elimination of slavery so it also leads to the elimination of a system oppressive to women.

Also, counterbalancing Paul's women-stay-in-the-background instructions is his clear statement on equality in Christ: "there are no more distinctions between Jew and Greek, slave and free, male or female, but you are all one in Christ" (Galations 3, 28).

Jesus, too, far from silencing women, entrusted the women at the tomb with the role of being the first proclaimers of the Gospel—the good news that the Savior lives.

On the occasion of the International Women's Year, Pope Paul reiterated a ringing statement in Vatican II's *Decree on the Apostolate of the Laity* (No. 9): "Since in our times women have an ever more active share in the whole life of society, it is very important that they participate more widely also in the various fields of the Church's apostolate."

It is in this spirit that women have been designated extraordi-

nary ministers of communion as well as given a variety of
other liturgical roles in the 1970 Vatican instruction, *Liturgiae
Instaurationes.* It says: "Women may:
• Proclaim the Scripture readings, with the exception of
  the Gospel.
• Offer the intentions for the Prayer of the Faithful. . . .
• Give the explanatory comments to help the people's
  understanding of the service. . . ."

As Archbishop Joseph L. Bernardin, president of the U.S.
bishops, asserted, "The Church will suffer, indeed it will be
betrayed, if women are given only a secondary place in its
life and mission."

 They've Downgraded the Real Presence!

**They've pushed Jesus right off the main altar and hidden him
in some corner. They've put benediction in mothballs.**

It is true that Rome has "highly recommended" that the Holy
Eucharist be reserved in a special chapel rather than on the
main altar. But the purpose for this is not to downgrade the
Blessed Sacrament or the Real Presence.

Rather than push Jesus off the main altar, the Church wants us
to focus on his presence there in new ways: Christ's presence
there in the *people* assembled in his name; his presence in the
word being proclaimed in the Scripture readings and homily;
his presence in the *priest* and *especially in the bread and wine
newly consecrated at that very sacrifice.*

With the tabernacle on the main altar our attention is too
easily diverted from the act of celebration taking place to the
reserved presence of the Lord in the tabernacle. Hence our
attention is divided. The Church feels that at this moment our
attention should be less on Christ's reserved presence than on
his presence in the Eucharist being celebrated and in his action
in our celebrating, in our giving thanks, in our sharing and
eating, and in our *coming together to build community
through the Mass.*

Therefore, the Church is not seeking to downgrade the Real
Presence or discourage Benediction. As fervently as ever, the
Church invites and encourages us to visit and pray before the
Blessed Sacrament. What the Church is trying to do is improve
our eucharistic devotion by simply *separating* our devotion to
the reserved presence from the Mass itself so that our attention
is not divided or confused.

 Social Justice Doesn't Belong at Mass!

**Why don't they put *religion* back into the pulpit and cut out
the politics they call social justice? Let the United Nations
solve the problem of world hunger; the Church should be
saving souls.**

True—religion belongs in the pulpit. But then the pursuit of
justice is at the very heart of religion. Isaiah taught that the
kind of piety and religion that God wanted was: "releasing
those bound unjustly, untying the thongs of the yoke, setting free the oppressed. . ." (Isaiah, 58, 6).

Jesus described his mission as "setting the downtrodden free"
(Luke 4, 18), and the 1971 World Synod of Bishops saw
working for justice as an essential or "constitutive dimension
of the preaching of the Gospel."

"Christ came to redeem the whole man, body and soul,"
asserts Cardinal John Krol of Philadelphia. "Thus the Church
is properly concerned with eradicating such temporal evils as
hunger and poverty, and oppression in all its forms, for these
are nothing else than concrete expressions of sin. The Church
is concerned with building a just social and political order."

In his 1975 document on *Evangelization in the Modern World*,
Pope Paul stated that the salvation proclaimed by Christ includes a "liberation from everything that oppresses man" and
that "the Church. . .has the duty to proclaim the liberation
[from famine, disease, poverty] of millions of human beings,
many of whom are her own children—the duty of assisting the
birth of this liberation, of giving witness to it, of ensuring

"I don't come to Church to hear about love and justice!"

that it is complete. This is not foreign to evangelization."

But the Pope warned about putting politics in the pulpit in so far as the Church's message of liberation should not be reduced to the merely temporal or political order. In other words, the homily at Mass should not be a platform for one's purely political preferences and must remain independent of manipulation by political parties. It is true that the pulpit is not the place for partisan politics, but a concern for social justice is an integral part of religion.

The Sacrifice Has Been Demoted!

They've downplayed Christ's sacrifice and reduced the Mass to a meal.

The Church still sees the Mass as a sacrifice. "The Lord's sacrifice is offered in the Eucharist in an unbloody and sacramental manner," clearly asserts Vatican II (*Decree on the Ministry and Life of Priests*, No. 2). No one has weakened our belief that Christ's redemptive offering of himself to the Father is made present in each Mass. Indeed we link ourselves in the Mass with Christ's sacrifice—a perfect sacrifice which alone has power to save us.

In recent years the Church has reminded us in new accents that the Mass is also a meal. Formerly, when the priest still had his back to the people, the altar sometimes seemed more like a sacrificial platform than a meal table. Also the fact that both priest and people faced the same way gave us the feeling that we were offering solemn sacrifice and prayers to a God "out there" beyond priest and congregation.

When the Church moved the altar forward and made it appear more like a table and had the priest face the community, we began getting a new feeling about the Mass and about God. Catholics did not discard the notion of sacrifice but simply put it more consciously in the context of a meal, much like Jesus did at the Last Supper—a meal which told us what the sacrifice was all about, namely the achievement of unity between God and his people. This also colored our feelings about God. Instead of focusing on him "out there," we began perceiving him more as being in our midst and in the interaction among priest and people.

 The Sign of Peace Is Phony!

It's hypocritical to shake hands with some total stranger who'll likely run you over in the parking lot.

The Sign of Peace in itself is no absolute proof or indication that this group of people has achieved perfect love and unity. It is simply a gesture of good will and reconciliation, a manifestation that we are willing and trying to be brothers and sisters.

The gesture of peace is strongly encouraged by the highest authorities of the Church. Pope Paul promulgated the instruction which urges and describes this gesture as follows: "The rite of peace: before they share in the same bread the people express their love for one another and beg for peace and unity in the Church and with all mankind" (*General Instruction for the Roman Missal*, No. 56).

Often we hesitate to reach out to others—whether that means a handshake, a smile, or sharing an inner feeling—until we fully trust the other person or the group involved. Until the trust level is perfect, we feel, we cannot risk a gesture of sharing. This may be an understandable human feeling, but if everyone waited until everyone else had perfect love or showed perfect courtesy in the parking lot, all human progress would grind to a halt. Human life would be paralyzed. Had Jesus waited until his followers were perfectly worthy before he handed over his Body and Blood to them, the first Eucharist would never have gotten off the ground.

As Father Joseph Champlin observes about the rite of peace, "To insist on perfect peace and justice before we celebrate is to expect the kingdom of the Lord before it appears. . . . If we postpone the sign of peace until all parishioners are reconciled, full of love and in harmony with one another, then I fear we will never see this gesture at Sunday Mass."

 Now why the different bread!

The new bread they sometimes use makes lots of crumbs and is hard to swallow.

Over the centuries the bread of the Eucharist got reduced to the thin coin-shaped wafer that to some eyes looks more like a paper disc than a piece of bread. Someone has commented, tongue in cheek, that it takes a greater leap of faith to believe the host is bread than to believe it is the Body of Christ!

Jesting aside, the Church considers it to be of "capital importance that the faithful easily understand the sacramental signs" (Vatican II, *Liturgy*, No. 59).

Thus in the *Order of the Mass*, Rome states "The nature of the sign demands that the material for the Eucharistic celebration appear as actual food. The Eucharistic bread, even though unleavened, should therefore be made in such a way that the priest can break it and distribute the parts to at least some of the faithful" (No. 283).

One reason Jesus chose such common household signs of bread and wine is that they would not seem threatening or frightening to us. After all who's afraid of a loaf of bread! Yet somehow over the years we have become terrified of making bread crumbs or touching with our teeth or hands what was given as food. Without losing our reverence for the Body of the Lord, we should not be upset with the new bread, or even with the crumbs, or the practice of chewing it, or with the Church's sincere efforts to make the Eucharistic meal look more like a meal.

 10 **There's No Time Left to Pray!**

They've got you saying things, listening to readers and commentators, singing bouncy songs. There's no time left for *me and God*.

Salvation is an interpersonal and community event. God never overlooks the individual but he has always saved his people *as a group*. He calls *his people* out of Egypt. It is as a people that he leads them through the desert or back from exile.

Certainly Jesus went after the lost sheep, but his purpose was precisely to form one flock. He indicated that salvation will not be complete until the whole flock is gathered together. Jesus longed to celebrate the Passover—the Last Supper—*with his disciples.* Bread was shared and psalms were sung together.

Thus the model of liturgical celebration that Jesus observed
and instituted was not that of rugged individualism but of
community celebration. He taught us to pray *"our* Father,"
not merely *"my* Father." This is not to say an individual is
not to pray alone to God—not at all. Jesus did that often,
and the Church wants places set aside in the Mass where there
is time to pray quietly and privately in God's presence.

But the Church is also reminding us unceasingly that we are
meant to help save each other and that we don't come to
salvation alone but as a people. The Church is always gently
nudging us to break through the shell of our egos and even
the walls of our parish Church and look at the larger salvation.
Mass prayers are continually prodding us to think bigger—to
embrace the whole Church, to include the Pope and bishops,
other cultures and searching people everywhere, East and
West—even our brothers and sisters of other centuries. The
Church seems to be saying: "Look, no one of us is going to
reach complete salvation until the whole flock reaches it
together."

Yes, the Mass should allow sufficient time for my personal
relationship to God, but it must also encourage shared prayer
and common celebration of the truth—and the good news—
that God wants us to come to salvation together.

Questions for Discussion

1. How does the Church recognize the variety of prayer styles in today's liturgical celebrations?

2. Father Joseph Champlin sees the Church returning to a better balance between silence and participation. What changes can you see that support or contradict this statement?

3. Why is participation in the Eucharist a "right and duty" of the laity?

4. Besides the pulpit message, can you suggest other ways that the Catholic Church could use to instruct its members about the social and political order?

5. How have the changes in design and gestures in the liturgy emphasized that the Mass is a communal meal?

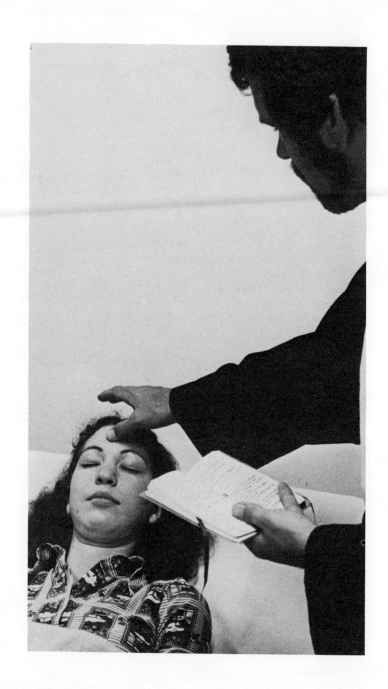

The New Rite of Anointing the Sick

by Barbara Beckwith

Let's say you're in the hospital. You're having stomach problems and tests are being done. The chaplain comes in. Which of the two following questions would you rather hear him ask:

- "Helen (John), would you like to receive the last rites?" or
- "Would you like us to pray for your healing?"

No doubt the second question would be more appealing. In any case, the change in attitude conveyed by the second question reflects a shift in the Church's understanding of the "Sacrament of the Sick" since Vatican II.

Many of us have not yet made this shift—at least, not completely. Father Gerald Niklas, chaplain at Good Samaritan

Hospital in Cincinnati and co-author of *Ministry to the
Hospitalized*, sees many people who still perceive Anointing
as "last rites" and resist or postpone the sacrament. "It takes
a long time to alter an idea they have had implanted for 50
years. . . . Intellectually they know better. But on a gut level
and in times of somewhat serious illness they revert to the
teachings of their grade school days," he observes.

The Stress Is on Healing

The new ritual for this most misunderstood and neglected
of the seven sacraments attempts to correct some of these
negative attitudes. The ritual was completed in 1972 by the
Vatican Congregation for Divine Worship. The English text is
official but provisional in America. Further changes in wording and instructions may yet be made by the U.S. Bishops'
Committee on the Liturgy.

Like the new rite for Penance, this new rite for Anointing is
not all that different from the old one. Primarily it's a matter
of reorientation and emphasis.

Healing is stressed over forgiveness of sins, evident immediately
in the change of wording for the actual anointing: the petition
is no longer to forgive the sins committed by each sense but to
"help you with the grace of the Holy Spirit" and to "save you
and raise you up." The suggested prayer that precedes the laying on of hands directly asks for healing: "Give life and health
to our brother/sister on whom we lay our hands in your name."
Other prayers and Scripture readings can be used to mention
healing when appropriate, for example, not stressing it for a
96-year-old suffering his third stroke but appropriate for a
29-year-old having exploratory surgery for cancer. The rite
itself contains a greater variety of Scripture and prayer texts
for just such flexibility.

A New Name

The most basic change of all is the name change. Sometimes a
rose is not a rose when called by another name. In the *Constitu-*

tion on the Liturgy, #73, the Second Vatican Council gave "Extreme Unction" or "Last Anointing" a more fitting description: "Anointing of the Sick."

This change is more than a word game: it indicates a whole

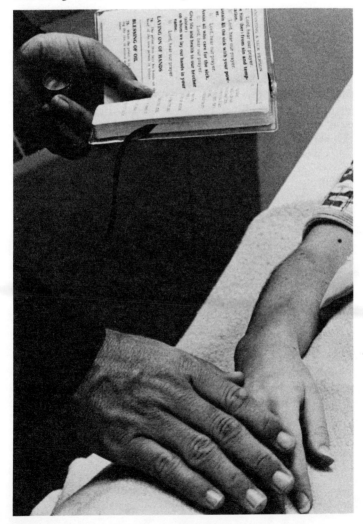

new attitude toward the sacrament. The former emphasis on "last" capitalized on the fear of imminent death. The new stress on sickness recognizes the obstacle that illness poses to a Christian's faith. We can talk about the nobility of suffering, but "more often it angers and confuses," says Leonard Foley, O.F.M., in *Signs of Love*. A University of Freiburg professor Dr. Adolf Knauber calls every serious illness a critical situation for the Christian with salvation or damnation at stake. The sick Christian must contend with bodily pain, mental depression, isolation, temptations to impatience and boredom, darkness and despair.

While death is not the focus of the sacrament, it is still an important backdrop to it. While *your* sickness is not a punishment for *your* personal sins, sickness in general is related to Original Sin. Death came into this world as a result of sin, and sickness is death's corollary and reminder.

Anointing is a sign of Christ's conquering death. In the midst of *your* illness the Church wants to reassure *you* that Christ triumphed over death and sickness. Anointing then associates our moments of illness with Christ's own suffering and unites us to Christ. It is an encounter with the saving Christ.

The Church isn't a mortuary—she is concerned about the living. She wants to bring the presence of Christ to those who need spiritual, mental and physical comfort in a time of trial and isolation.

Who Should Receive the Sacrament?

Therefore, Anointing is not just a sacrament for those at the point of death. "As soon as any of the faithful *begins* to be in danger of death from sickness or old age, the fitting time for him to receive this sacrament has *certainly already arrived*" (*Constitution on the Liturgy*, #73). [Emphasis added.]

In concrete terms, this means patients dangerously ill or about to undergo major surgery, the elderly debilitated by old age even if no dangerous illness or immediate danger of death is present, and seriously ill children who have sufficient understanding to be comforted by the sacrament should be anointed. In some hospitals Anointing is offered automatically to those over 60.

The seriously ill who have lost consciousness or the use of reason should also be anointed if in a conscious state they would have requested it. The sacrament may be repeated during the same illness if the patient suffers a relapse or his condition becomes more critical.

"A prudent or probable judgment regarding the seriousness of the illness suffices; scrupulosity should be avoided," insists the *Study Text II on Anointing and Pastoral Care of the Sick*, published by the U.S. Bishops' Committee on the Liturgy.

The practice used to be to anoint those already pronounced dead on the assumption that the soul might not have left the body yet. The new rite specifies that the certainly dead are not to be anointed because they have no chance of recovery. The priest should pray for the dead person, asking God to receive him into his kingdom. Chaplain Father Niklas finds most grieving families are content to have the priest offer a prayer for the dead person and the family after they have had explained to them the purpose of the sacrament and why Anointing is no longer appropriate.

Does Anointing Promise Healing?

The purpose of Anointing, like that of all sacraments, is to make visible (or "sensible") an act of Christ through his Church. In this sacrament Christ's "grace-full" act is to strengthen the sick person with a deeper sharing of his life. God in his grace affects the whole person, not just the "soul." In light of new findings in psychology and medicine regarding the intricate interworkings of mind and body, it should not be surprising that a change in bodily health can be effected.

With the old emphasis on forgiveness of sin, we had no doubt about the efficacy of the sacrament. The new rite certainly suggests that the sacrament *promises* healing, yet we have all seen people who have been anointed and died. Does the rite *promise* healing? The answer to this question involves a hard look at Jesus' healing ministry.

"Every time a sick person came to him in faith, Jesus healed that person," insists Francis P. MacNutt, O.P., in his comprehensive work, *Healing*. Jesus "did not divide man, as we so often do, into a soul to be saved and healed and a body that is to suffer and remain unhealed," Father MacNutt says. Sickness of the body was part of the kingdom of Satan that Jesus had come to destroy. Jesus' healing miracles were signs of the coming of the kingdom of God, mighty signs that announce and usher in this kingdom.

The problem is that real healing does not always and exclusively mean *physical* recovery; the body is not always where the sick hurt most. Anointing involves an act of faith that God will heal—now or in the resurrected body. Anointing guarantees the person who receives it in faith a victory over illness by getting well or by overcoming the spiritual obstacles sickness poses or by a good Christian death. Any of these alternatives, even death, is a victory and a healing to a true Christian.

In his book Father MacNutt speaks of four distinct kinds of healing: healing from sickness of our spirit, caused by personal sin, which demands a prayer of repentance; inner healing ("healing of memories") for emotional problems and hurts of our past; physical healing for the sickness of our bodies, caused by disease or accidents; and deliverance from demonic oppression.

Considered from this wider perspective, it is clear that Anointing of the Sick does bring healing if we cooperate with it in faith. But this is not some kind of quasi-magic. So much depends on the faith of the sick person: "This faith is important for the minister and particularly for the one who receives it. The sick man will be saved by his faith and the faith of the Church which looks back to the death and resurrection of Christ, the source of the sacrament's power, and looks forward to the future kingdom which is pledged in the sacraments" (*Rite of Anointing*, Introduction, #7).

The Rite's Symbols

Besides the words, the nonverbal symbols of the sacrament also convey the notion of healing. The laying on of the hands expresses concern and strength through the sense of touch. The new ritual has restored this ancient gesture, mistakenly omitted from the old ritual.

Olive oil remains an important visible element of the sacrament, although other vegetable oil is permitted wherever obtaining olive oil has been a problem. Vegetable oil is now frequently used in the States.

"The use of oil in Anointing of the Sick is perhaps the most immediately intelligible liturgical use of oil for contemporary man who frequently applies soothing oil to the ailing members of his body," comments *Study Text II*. In keeping with the revised liturgies of Baptism and Confirmation, the oil applied to the sick person's forehead and hands need not be removed as if it were a harmful substance, thus reinforcing its healing symbolism.

The practice of anointing the sick with oil appears to have been a Palestinian custom, which was taken over by Jesus and his followers: "So they [the Twelve] set off to preach repentance; and they cast out many devils, and *anointed many sick people with oil* and cured them" (Mark 6:13). [Emphasis added.]

In the Latin Church the blessing of the oil is normally reserved to the bishop, who blesses it at Holy Thursday's Chrism Mass. However, the new ritual permits the priest to bless his own oil in cases of "true necessity" and when the blessing prayer over the oil would be instructive.

Except in urgent cases, the rite itself should involve some degree of liturgical planning, determining which readings and prayers are appropriate and, where feasible, music. Themes of healing, peace and paschal mystery should prevail. The petitions and Our Father could easily be sung. When done properly, music can enrich the *celebration* aspect of the rite.

69

Getting the Christian Community Involved

The *Constitution on the Liturgy* of Vatican II stressed that "liturgical functions are not private functions, but are celebrations of the Church" (#26). The new rite of Anointing is no exception, with communal celebrations rather than solitary ones suggested as the norm. The Anointing of the Sick should normally be celebrated in the presence of the person's relatives and friends, who actively participate by praying, responding, reading, singing, etc.

This participation allows the sick person to sense in the sacrament not only the concern of Christ to help him but also the concern of other Christians who are in effect saying, "We're all for you, we're pulling for you."

For one family the new rite of Anointing was combined with a home Mass, just prior to the father's open-heart surgery. It renewed their sense of family and of Church at a very critical time in their lives.

But sometimes communal celebration is not practical, admits hospital chaplain Father Niklas: "Sometimes the sacrament is urgent and the family is not there; sometimes in a large hospital it isn't always possible to set a time when the family can be present."

There also exists the possibility of anointing several sick Christians within the same ceremony in a church or chapel. Group anointings may be celebrated with Mass after the Liturgy of the Word or in a Communion service or as a distinct rite, similar to the one introduced at Lourdes with great success. Parishes may hold communal celebrations of the sacrament at regular intervals.

"One of the best ways to reduce the anxiety of people who still consider the sacrament a rite for the dying is for them to participate in group anointings at church," Father Niklas has noticed. They see the sick who can walk to church or at least come in wheelchairs—ill people who are not breathing their last breath—receiving the sacrament and hearing the petitions for their recovery. "This is more effective help than a sermon because you see it with your eyes, you talk to people who have been anointed," he says.

Ministry Doesn't Stop With the Sacrament

The rite makes it quite clear that ministry to the sick does not stop with the sacrament of Anointing. "When rightly understood, the priestly-human visit to the sick can itself, without any liturgical action, become an encounter with Christ," Dr. Knauber says. Christians visiting the sick are also *sacraments* of Christ because they bring his presence with them. This insight should enrich the ministry of those who visit the sick.

The rite stresses that visiting the sick is not only for priests but for all Christians (#42). There is no prescribed ritual for visiting the sick; rather the rite urges all Christians to share their faith by praying with the sick and strengthening them with their presence and support.

An Invitation to Meet the Healing Savior

The reform of the rite and the stress on total ministry to the sick are intended to relate to the real lives and needs of Christians. The sick who suffer loneliness, isolation and a sense of uselessness in a pragmatic society that has no time for non-producers need encouragement and support in their faith.

To counter the sick person's feelings of loneliness, the revised rite proposes communal prayer with friends and relatives or others to be anointed. To counter their feelings of dependency, the new rite offers a call to self-growth, faith and conversion.

The sacrament of Anointing should be approached joyfully. It is an opportunity to meet the healing, comforting, loving, compassionate Savior in a tangible way and in a way which expresses his concern for your total healing. Even if he does not take away your sickness, even if he does not make you young again, he will give you his strength. He will help you understand the meaning of your age and illness—and he will empower you to bear it with patience and love. In more ways than one, he will raise you up.

71

How to Prepare for the Anointing of the Sick

To be *fully* celebrated, the sacrament should take place at the *earliest* possible occasion at the *beginning* of a serious illness. To ensure this, the new rite asks priests to encourage Catholics, both publicly and privately, to request the sacrament on their own initiative rather than postpone it. Family and friends of the sick person and those who take care of him or her should inform the pastor or hospital or nursing home chaplain if his sickness worsens.

If the sacrament is to be celebrated at home or in a hospital, it is proper to clear a table near the sickbed where the priest may set down the pyx containing the Blessed Sacrament. (The Anointing rite often includes Communion.) The table may be covered with a white cloth to indicate reverence and welcome for the Blessed Sacrament.

The old ritual suggested a cross and two lighted candles on the table; this still sets a proper atmosphere. The candles may be left unlit if oxygen is being used. A glass or bowl of water is also mentioned so that the priest may wipe his fingers of the oil if he wishes. A glass of water and a teaspoon is sometimes suggested in case the person receiving Communion would have trouble swallowing the Host.

The priest brings with him the blessed oil and, usually, the holy water used in the sprinkling at the beginning.

If the sacrament of Penance is desired, the priest should hear the confession of the sick person before the celebration of Anointing, if possible. Otherwise a penitential rite takes place during the introductory rite.

The priest should explain the sacrament to those participating before and at various times during the ritual. Often he will indicate the type of response expected, e.g., "Amen" or "Lord, hear our prayer" or "I confess to almighty God. . . ." Sometimes he may distribute a pamphlet so those participating may follow the ritual more easily.

72

Questions for Discussion

1. What does the name change—from "Extreme Unction" to "Anointing of the Sick"—indicate about the Church's attitude?

2. How is anointing an act of faith?

3. Who should receive the sacrament?

4. How do the non-verbal symbols of the sacrament convey the idea of healing?

5. How should the sick person and his/her family and friends prepare for Anointing of the Sick?

New Perspectives on Christian Marriage

by Karen Hurley

Marriage has always been the butt of humor, high and low.
TV comics could depend on jokes about nagging wives or
bumbling husbands to trigger knowing laughter in their audi-
ences. Poking fun at the comedies and tragedies of married
life only further cemented people's understanding of marriage as the fullness of the human condition—for better or
for worse.

But marriage is no longer a laughing matter. The statistics
sober us: over a million American marriages ended in divorce
or separation last year. Mentions of marriage today usually
grow out of cynicism or fear, not humor. The cynic quips:
"Who needs marriage? A piece of paper doesn't mean anything." The fearful ask: "But won't marriage destroy our

love—and us in the process?''

Marriage is fast losing its taken-for-granted status in our society. A whole new set of questions is being raised about marriage. And in the face of these questions Catholics must try to
define anew what marriage means.

Some New Questions

1) "Will they *ever* get married?"

   Meg Greenfield, writing in her *Newsweek* column, described
the dilemma facing an increasing number of parents: a son or
daughter who is living with a member of the opposite sex
"without benefit of marriage," as the old expression goes.
She sympathizes with the practical problems these parents
face—not the least of which is deciding what to call the
"live-in" in normal conversation and personal introductions.
After considering the various terms that might be used (e.g.,
my daughter's "friend," "boyfriend," "lover," "fiance")
and discarding each as inadequate, she suggests a term of her
own creation: *spose*, as in "Meet my daughter's spose, Jim."

   This term has two important points to recommend it, she
feels. First, it is closely related to *spouse* and therefore gives
some suggestion of the quasi-nuptial nature of the relationship.
Second, and most importantly, it articulates the ever-present
question on the concerned parent's mind: "*Spose* they will
ever get married?"

   Not too many years ago parents' biggest worry was that
their children would jump into marriage too soon, or to the
wrong person. The times have changed!

2) "Why get married *first*?"

   Some of the young adults in "live-in" arrangements respond
to the question "Will you *ever* get married" by answering,
"Maybe." But they go on to raise the further question: "Why
now? We need to try this relationship on for size, to see if we
are really compatible before we make any permanent commitments, before we bring any children into the world." Aware of
the soaring divorce rates, they do not want to become just
another set of statistics.

3) "Why get married *at all*?"

Others would take issue with the very notion of a permanent commitment or a legal bond. They suspect that one cannot honestly say "Till death do us part." They choose instead to say, "Until our love dies."

So, they ask, "Why get married at all?" They refuse to bind someone—or themselves—to a relationship once the growing stops, once the love dies.

4) "Why *stay* married?"

Those already married find it increasingly easy to ask "Why stay married?" If a marriage relationship is having serious difficulties, or if it just isn't particularly satisfying any more, the old reasons (the children, finances, what the neighbors will think) don't seem very convincing. Besides, it almost seems that society now puts the burden of proof on those who stay married rather than on those who decide to split.

Many Catholics see the multiplication of questions like the above in our society and even in their own families as the most significant change on the marriage scene today. Another change, however, accompanies this question-raising. Because marriage is no longer a taken-for-granted in our society, more and more people are forced to explore, redefine and rediscover the very meaning of marriage. Such a change has many *positive* implications for those concerned with the future of Christian marriage.

What *Kind* of Marriage?

Questions like those above about whether to get married or stay married give many the impression that marriage has fallen on hard times. Maybe a more accurate way of describing the present situation, though, would be to say that our general social consensus on what marriage means has broken down. Must it really be "forever"? Must it include the possibility of children? Does it depend on some form of sex-role stereotyping with husband as head and wife as heart?

People are struggling in different ways to define what they want in a stable, loving relationship. Many people, while not yet certain about what they *do* want, are very definite about what they *don't* want: the kind of marriages they see all around them.

One of the most widely-known attempts at re-defining marriage is the book *Open Marriage* by Nena and George O'Neill. The authors of this best-seller report the following as the most common criticism of traditional marriage by those who are in it, those who have gotten out of it, and those who are avoiding getting into it: that it closes people in on themselves and locks them into roles that stifle their personal growth.

Because the O'Neills feel that "the psychological and structural imperatives for marriage are strong," they are unwilling to give up on marriage completely. They propose a new kind of marriage which they call "open marriage." They describe it as "an honest and open relationship between two people, based on the equal freedom and identity of both partners," involving "a verbal, intellectual and emotional commitment to the right of each to grow as an individual within the marriage."

Other alternative models of marriage are suggested by occasional articles in *Ms.* magazine on how to write a feminist marriage contract. Such efforts point up the new quest for a better *kind* of marriage.

The question today is not merely whether to marry or not, or whether to stay married or not. People are also asking: If we want to marry, or if we want to stay married, what *kind* of marriage shall we make it? What *kind* of commitment are we willing to live?

"What kind of marriage do we want? That is the heart of the matter," insists Edward R. Dufresne in his book *Partnership: Marriage and the Committed Life*. "The expanded number of choices within marriage has given us a sense that partnership should not be something that happens to us; it is something we create."

This is the bright side of all the new questioning about marriage in our culture. Not only is marriage being chosen with a greater degree of forethought and seriousness of purpose when chosen, but with a greater appreciation of the various types of commitments one could make, the various married life-styles one could embrace.

The growing popularity of Engaged Encounters and other local approaches to pre-marriage preparation (like Tobit Weekends in Indianapolis) indicate that while marriage may no longer be taken for granted, it is being taken *seriously.*

Developments in official policies regarding who can and cannot marry in the Catholic Church reflect this new concern for taking marriage seriously, but not for granted. A growing number of dioceses in the United States, most notably the dioceses in the state of New Jersey, are adopting common policies for determining when a couple is psychologically mature enough to enter a sacramental marriage and when a couple's commitment in fact constitutes a Christian commitment.

Covenant vs. Contract

Christian marriage is a *covenant,* not merely a *contract*—despite the fact that the Church frequently uses contract language in talking about sacramental marriage. As theologian Monika Hellwig says in her book *The Meaning of the Sacraments:* "Covenant is different from contract. In the latter there is an exchange of pledges or commitments to quite specific obligations which are spelled out beforehand so that each party to the contract knows exactly what is involved and what his responsibilities are. But in a covenant of alliance or friendship, the commitment is open-ended. It is a pledge of personal loyalty to be sustained in changing and unpredictable circumstances."

Because of this covenant nature of Christian marriage we have come to see it as a sacrament. Those who enter Christian marriage promise to let their covenant to each other be a concrete sign, day in and day out, of God's covenant with us. They promise to let their fidelity to each other, despite changing circumstances, be a sign of God's unwavering fidelity to us.

79

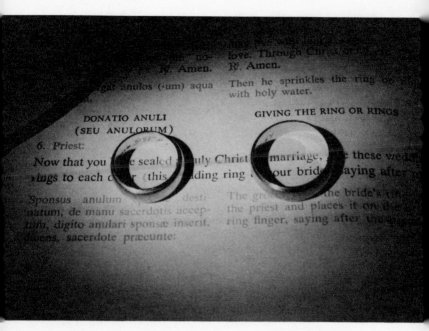

When presented with these alternatives, it might seem that no
one would choose anything but a covenant relationship. In
contrast, a contract marriage might seem inhuman, coldly
calculating and legalistic.

But it's not that black and white. Some, like the O'Neills,
would argue for the opposite point of view. They see the
ideas that marriage "will last forever," "that it means total
commitment," "that fidelity is a true measure of the love
you have for one another," "that sacrifice is a true measure
of love," as "unrealistic expectations, unreasonable ideals
and mythological beliefs" that are dehumanizing in a marriage
relationship. They urge couples, therefore, to be specific in
spelling out more *realistic* terms for their marriage *contract*.

Of course there is some sound psychology behind the O'Neills'
view. Some of the traditional Christian language about marriage
can unwittingly reinforce unrealistic, "romantic" views of mar-

riage which deserve serious criticism. For example, it can happen that the traditional emphasis on children as an important fulfillment in marriage leads some to the erroneous conclusion that a baby will solve their marriage problems. Or our traditional language about spouses "belonging" to each other can reinforce immature expectations that spouses should spend *all* spare time together, or single-handedly fulfill all the other person's needs.

Christians *Can* Say "Forever"

But there is another type of "realism" in the open marriage view that doesn't fit with the Christian vision. Open marriage is ultimately open to the possibility that marriage may end, that two people may grow in different directions, and that this isn't the end of the world.

This position may appear realistic in terms of current divorce rates. But Christian tradition takes serious issue with this supposed realism. As Hellwig points out: "Biblical faith. . .is concerned with transforming the world as we now have it with all the apparently inescapable consequences of evil deeds into the reign of God. . . . Therefore, each sacramental celebration carries something of this thrust toward the realization of the apparently impossible."

The sacrament of marriage carries this "thrust toward the apparently impossible" in the unconditional commitment man and woman make to each other in their marriage covenant. This emphasis on the permanence of marriage is an ideal that is essential to the very notion of Christian marriage.

Even those Catholics like Msgr. Stephen Kelleher (*Divorce and Remarriage for Catholics?*) who would like to see the Church relax the severity of present marriage *laws* don't question the importance of this *ideal* in defining sacramental marriage. They argue, rather that the Western Church should follow more closely the tradition of the Eastern Churches in admitting that people fall short of the ideal and that this failure must be recognized.

81

But such "realism" is of an entirely different nature than admitting that one shouldn't strive for the ideal in the first place and firmly commit oneself to living it out in married life.

How "Open" Is Christian Marriage?

The quest for personal growth is an all-consuming passion in our present culture. Personal growth centers and personal growth institutes are springing up all over the country. It is no surprise that the book *Open Marriage* focuses on creating a marriage model that provides the greatest opportunity for personal growth for both spouses.

The big surprise about *Open Marriage*, however, is the role it assigns *commitment* in fostering personal growth. The O'Neills are all for it! They attack the prevailing myth that commitments limit a person's opportunities for growth, that "tying yourself down" is bad, that you must "keep all your options open" in order to grow. They argue for some form of marriage commitment because it "still provides the only framework in which people can find the stability in which to experience the full intimacy of a one-to-one relationship" and, they continue, such intimacy is a necessary prerequisite for significant personal growth.

In contrast to the present cultural suspicions about commitment-making, this reaffirmation of the marriage commitment may seem like good news for Christians. And to some extent, it certainly is good news. But the way open marriage relates commitment to personal growth stands in some tension with the Catholic tradition's understanding of the marriage ideal. It all boils down to a conflict between a view of human nature that is basically individualistic and a Christian view that emphasizes personal interdependence.

The open marriage ideal says: "Make commitments, yes. They are definitely necessary for growth. You never live deeply or intimately unless you do commit yourself." Up to this point, the Christian understanding of personal growth would find no argument.

But the open marriage view goes on to say: "The way to judge the value of any commitment is whether it continues to keep you growing. When you stop growing in one relationship, maybe it is time to move on." In other words, the O'Neills say, commitments are valuable only insofar as they serve our individual growth goals, only as long as they help us become the kind of person *we* think we should be becoming.

The Christian Alternative

The Christian ideal suggests a radical alternative: that none of us really knows in advance the best direction for our personal growing. Christians entering marriage ideally decide to allow themselves to grow in an *unknown* direction but a direction that is related to each other. They trust themselves to the basic goodness of their commitment and pledge to grow in whatever direction that commitment pushes and prods them.

Instead of measuring a marriage commitment in terms of preconceived notions of personal growth, the Christian decides to measure personal growth in terms of a marriage commitment. He chooses to ask questions like these to determine how well he is growing: "How faithful am I to my spouse, to my marriage covenant?" "How willing am I to respond to a Lord who calls me through my marriage commitment?"

The open marriage view of commitment and personal growth leads to that most peculiar phenomenon of our time: the friendly divorce. People who share the open marriage model can decide at some point, with a certain amount of dispassion that, since they are now growing in opposite directions, it is best to call the commitment off so they don't stand in the way of each other's development. Beneath such a view of commitment there remains a fundamental individualism that cannot be reconciled with the Christian paradox that one finds one's self only by losing one's self in the service of another.

Christian marriage is *open* to growth, but the kind of growth that is fundamentally determined by a relationship to another.

83

Christians in marriage commit themselves to a shared future that will challenge them to grow in ways they cannot even imagine as they begin their covenant together.

Such a radical commitment to living a common future depends on good communication between spouses and a very high degree of common caring and sensitivity. The popularity of Christian marriage enrichment programs like the Marriage Encounter point up the tremendous need Christian couples feel to keep opening their marriages to further opportunities to grow—both together and in relation to the wider community.

What Answers Are There?

There is no end in sight to the contemporary questioning of marriage. Catholics can take some comfort in realizing that this questioning can lead those who choose marriage to a fuller and more Christian understanding of marriage. This *general* observation, however, gives only slight solace when the questions are directed *at us* by people we know and love. We need specific responses.

There are some definite things we can *say* to the questions about marriage:
- *Commitment is important. No one grows without it.*
- *Personal growth is a dangerous yardstick for measuring a marriage commitment.*
- *The Christian ideal of permanence is not unrealistic.*

Plus, there is something very definite we can *do*:
- *Married Christians can share the positive values in their own marriages.*

A painful aspect of the present questioning about marriage is the charge: "If marriage is so great and good for personal growth, why can't I name any happy marriages?"

But this seeming charge is really just another question—and a very *personal* question addressed to all the married people

85

within earshot: "Tell me, are *you* happy in your marriage?"
We are being asked to share the good things about our lives—
the things we can so easily forget to mention.

The most ardent haranguer against marriage can be trans-
formed into a receptive listener when someone speaks from
his or her married experience to say: "I worry about you and
Jim living together because *my own* marriage commitment
has been so important in freeing me to be me. I would like you
to have the same opportunity for a deeply challenging personal
relationship."

The questions raised at the beginning of this chapter don't have
any easy answers. But all married Catholics who are glad to be
married know some very important truths that need to be
shared—without moralizing or condemning or judging. We
have to believe that the fruitfulness of our Christian marriage
commitment can speak for itself; but we must be willing to
find the courage and take the time to share what we've experienced when we hear someone asking these new questions
about marriage.

Questions for Discussion

1. How does theologian Monika Hellwig distinguish between *covenant* and *contract*?

2. Explain how even a book like *Open Marriage* sees a value in commitment. Is "personal growth" the only measure for judging a marriage? Explain.

3. What common guidelines do you think should determine a couple's psychological readiness for marriage? What constitutes a Christian commitment to marriage?

4. What questions would you ask to measure your growth in your marriage?

5. What value is there in pre-marriage programs?

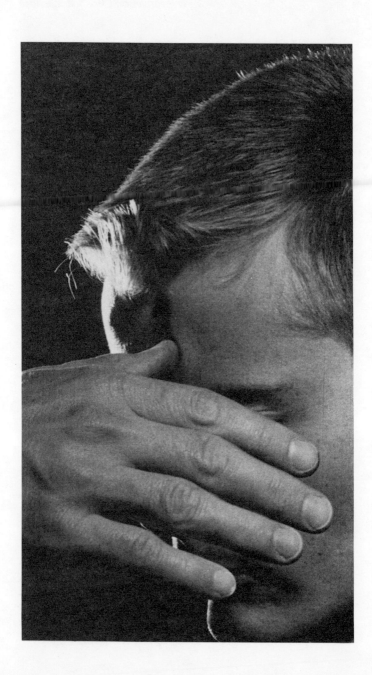

Lent and Penance Today

by Patrick McCloskey, O.F.M.

"Lent used to be very special," comment many Catholics these days. "Years ago in grade school we used to give up candy and compete to see who could raise more money to save pagan babies. Lent meant avoiding parties and movies and making the Stations of the Cross on Fridays. Once there was a strict Lenten fast; hardly anything is left of the old fast now. Lent used to mean something; now we are supposed to choose our own penances and nobody knows what Lent means."

There is no denying that Lenten practice and other penitential observances have changed for U. S. Catholics in the last few years. Many ask if the change has been for the better. This chapter will study that question and perhaps trigger some ideas for your observance of Lent and the general practice of penance.

In February of 1966, Pope Paul issued a document signaling a change in the Church's practice of penance. After saying that he felt obliged to remind Catholics of the important divine command to do penance, Pope Paul declared that the kingdom of God requires a change of heart—that inner conversion must accompany external penances.

What sort of penances should be practiced? "The Church insists," said Pope Paul, "that the virtue of penitence be exercised in persevering faithfulness to the duties of one's state in life, in the acceptance of the difficulties arising from one's work and from human coexistence, in a patient bearing of the trials of earthly life and of the utter insecurity which pervades it."

After commending the time-honored combination of prayer/fasting/charity as the "fundamental means of complying with the divine precept of penitence," Pope Paul established Ash Wednesday and Good Friday as days of fast and abstinence and the Fridays of Lent as days of abstinence.

In November of the same year the U. S. bishops followed up on the Pope's document with a pastoral statement which described Lent as the "principal season of penance in the Church year" and urgently asked that Catholics "make of Lent a period of special penitential observance." The bishops recommended that Catholics continue voluntarily to observe some acts of penance on all Fridays of the year; Friday abstinence was still recommended but it was not required by law except during Lent. Fridays were also singled out as days for volunteer charity. "It would bring great glory to God and good to souls," they wrote, "if Fridays found our people:
- doing volunteer work in hospitals
- visiting the sick
- serving the needs of the aged and the lonely
- instructing the young in the faith
- participating as Christians in community affairs
- and meeting our obligations to our families, our friends, our neighbors and our community, including our parishes, with special zeal. . . ."

90

Eating a tuna casserole on Friday might not be as penitential as visiting Uncle Jack in a nearby nursing home. Perhaps some of those old forms of penance were not as difficult as some of the suggested newer forms. After explaining the new regulations, the U. S. bishops said that if they are entered into with the proper spirit, they "will herald a new birth of loving faith and more profound penitential conversion, by both of which we become one with Christ, mature sons of God and servants of God's people." On that November 27, 1966, the Catholic Church in the U. S. entered a new age of penitential practice.

Why Change Anyway?

Neither Pope Paul nor the U. S. bishops intended to downplay the need for penance; on the contrary, both stressed it very strongly. But the Lenten fast and Friday abstinence were not necessarily the most effective means of practicing penance. The Church used to emphasize both the need for and the details of penance; now she chose to reaffirm the *need* for penance and leave the details up to the individual penitent.

Thus, if today there is less observance of Lent through external penance, shall we say the Church has given up on penance? I think it more accurate to say that *if* there is less penance, then individual Catholics have not sufficiently responded to the invitation to find a penitential practice expressive of their inner conversion.

The Church has not given up on penance. In fact, the time-honored trio of prayer, fasting and works of charity is recommended as much now as ever. And this chapter will explore what Catholics can do during Lent in each of these three areas.

Prayer Is a Pre-Condition

Prayer is the front-running penitential practice according to the Church's tradition. Is prayer a penance? Not in itself. But if the heart of penance is a deepening conversion to God's ways (*metanoia*), then prayer is the absolute pre-condition to real penance. Devout prayer warns against any formalism in penance—i.e., priding oneself on external observance for its own sake. In prayer we come to know the God we serve; without prayer our practice of penance is rooted in poor soil and is bound to be choked off by indifference.

Participating in that sphere of prayer known as liturgy thus becomes a vital part of this penitential season. Is your parish scheduling a weekday evening Mass during Lent? Could you attend? Have you joined in the Holy Week liturgy in past years? Have you attended the Easter Vigil, the highpoint of the liturgical year?

The private prayer of individual believers remains important. Perhaps during Lent you could clear out 15 minutes a day for a prayerful reading of the Bible, or consider beginning the practice of regular meditation, or pray the Stations of the Cross and the rosary.

Certainly Lent is the ideal time for examining the direction (or drift) of our lives and for asking God's forgiveness in confession. Recently the new rite of Penance was introduced throughout the U.S. The reformed ritual is thus available to the confessor and penitent. Also, there is an increased stress on the whole Church's involvement in the reconciliation of sinners; our return to wholeness affects our relationship not only with God but our fellow believers (the Church) as well. Very likely, your parish has already worked through Sunday homilies and special programs to acquaint Catholics with this new rite for Penance. Learning even more about the ritual and *celebrating* it could contribute to a fruitful, prayerful Lent.

Fasting: Altering Our Life-Styles

In the Church's tradition, this is the second way of penance. Pope Paul did not throw out fasting. Rather, he strongly recommended it in 1966. The motive for fasting is not to "punish" our bodies as evil, but rather to free ourselves from the control of unrestrained bodily desires. Pope Paul wrote, "Through 'corporal fasting' man regains strength and 'the wound inflicted on the dignity of our nature by intemperance

92

is cured by the medicine of a salutary abstinence.' " In the
U. S. bishops' pastoral of 1966, they stressed the need for
self-discipline regarding bodily comforts, such as alcohol.
Self-discipline is not a uniquely Christian virtue, but it is
required of Jesus' followers so that, through voluntary self-
denial, we may learn to follow the Lord whose acceptance
of the cross led from Good Friday to Easter Sunday.

In November of 1974, eight years after the Church removed
the obligation of the Lenten fast, the U. S. bishops responded
to the world food crisis by asking Catholics to fast at least
two days a week. The money saved could be contributed to
some food relief organization; this gave us a cue to the
broader meaning of fasting as related to generosity for others.

True Fasting—Setting Others Free

This, rather, is the fasting that I wish:
    releasing those bound unjustly,
    untying the thongs of the yoke;
Setting free the oppressed,
    breaking every yoke;
Sharing your bread with the hungry,
    sheltering the oppressed and the homeless;
Clothing the naked when you see them,
    and not turning your back on your own.
Then your light shall break forth like the dawn,
    and your wound shall quickly be healed;
Your vindication shall go before you,
    and the glory of the Lord shall be your rear guard.
Then you shall call, and the Lord will answer,
    you shall cry for help, and he will say,
    Here I am!

—Isaiah 58: 6—9A
New American Bible Translation

Another form of fasting is examining one's life-style for wasteful habits and for the tendency to uncritically satisfy advertising-induced "needs." Perhaps the U. S. bishops contributed significantly to our personal growth when they placed responsibility for choosing a penitential practice on our shoulders. Perhaps taking only one martini is a better penance than eating shrimp on Friday. Abstaining from the latest "necessity" may be better than two days of fasting.

Deepening our Catholic education may not strike us immediately as a form of fasting, but it could be seen as a related penitential practice. For taking time to expand our knowledge and invest the time and money needed is surely an exercise in self-discipline, in giving up one thing for the sake of another. So you might ask yourself: When did I last read a Catholic book or subscribe to a Catholic magazine? Is my parish offering adult education programs this Lent? Is there a lecture series in town? Do I read my diocesan newspaper? Does it carry the "Know Your Faith" series?

Time is a precious commodity for most people. Many of us feel we do not have enough of it or that too many demands are being made on us. But if time is precious to us, then it is a natural possibility for self-denial; it can be sacrificed for a higher good or the good of another.

For example, a friend of mine says that attending meetings is *the* modern form of penance. Obviously, not all meetings are productive or fun to attend, yet some things—community projects especially—require them. What is your involvement in community organizations or projects? Could you share more of your time? Many people complain about government these days; have you recently taken time to write to an elected official about something important to you? Has your parish or some nearby organization gotten involved in a world-food program? Could you make any contribution to such an effort?

Our time is limited, and we already have various family and work responsibilities. But somewhere along the line we have

to ask ourselves what the priorities are that determine our
use of time.

Works of Charity Have Modern Guises

The works of charity complete the triangle of time-honored
penitential practices. Today there are many people with various
needs; no one of us can feed all the hungry people in the world
or visit all the lonely people confined to their own homes or
apartments or nursing homes. No one of us can comfort all
those who are mourning. But each of us can perform some
act of charity for the benefit of another.

The Baltimore Catechism listed the chief corporal works of
mercy as: feeding the hungry; giving drink to the thirsty;
clothing the naked; visiting the imprisoned; sheltering the
homeless; visiting the sick; and burying the dead. The chief
spiritual works of mercy are: admonishing the sinner; instructing the ignorant; counseling the doubtful; comforting the sor-
rowful; bearing wrongs patiently; forgiving all injuries; and
praying for the living and the dead. These have not been
thrown out! Indeed, in 1966 when the U. S. bishops listed
possible voluntary Friday penances, they cited many of
these practices.

If you suspect that Catholics are not doing as much penance as
they did 15 years ago, consider some of the developments
since then:

- The Campaign for Human Development, sponsored by the
  U. S. bishops, has distributed $24 million for economic and
  social development programs since beginning in 1970. Each
  year the contributions have increased despite nationwide
  economic setbacks.
- Through the U. S. Catholic Conference, U. S. parishes have
  assisted in the resettlement of 53,000 Southeast Asian
  refugees from April through December, 1975.
- In 1975 Catholic Relief Services distributed $18.1 million,
  including $10.4 million raised by special collections for the
  aid of drought-stricken sections of the world.
- U. S. Catholics contributed $23.3 million to the Society for

95

the Propagation of the Faith in 1974 and $22.5 million in 1973.

- More and more Catholics are assisting in CCD instruction and serving on worship committees, parish councils and various other groups serving the local Church.
- Traditional groups such as Catholic Charities, the St. Vincent de Paul Society and the Legion of Mary have continued their efforts in the corporal and spiritual works of mercy. New groups like FISH continue to aid people physically and spiritually.

It seems that the question is not whether Catholicism has abandoned the works of mercy but whether I have joined in those efforts.

Lent: Time of Reconciliation

Above all, Lent provides a time for considering our life with God, for considering our following of Jesus. This season offers a perfect occasion for seeking renewal and reconciliation, the twin themes of the recently-completed Holy Year. Through that jubilee year Pope Paul hoped to promote personal reconciliation on four levels: with God, ourselves, each other and the whole created world. Speaking last year on reconciliation within the Church, Pope Paul asked all Catholics to "show themselves to be ever more docile disciples of the Lord, who makes reconciliation between us the condition for being forgiven by the Father (cf. Mark 11:26) and mutual charity the condition for being recognized as his disciples (cf. John 13: 35)."

Our Church leaders stress reconciliation. Through prayer, fasting and the works of charity we can aid that reconciliation. More concretely, perhaps we should be seeking reconciliation with one particular person. Can we make that first step? Can we promote any reconciliation between opposing groups? Pope Paul prayed not only for reconciliation but for an accompanying inner renewal especially in prayer, penitential practices and the use of the sacrament of penance. Lent can be a time of reconciliation if we make it so.

A Family Lent

Various books and pamphlets to promote a family observance of Lent are available. As a Lenten practice, could your family set aside a certain time to pray together? Could you read Bible stories to your small children? Some families enjoy celebrating the Passover meal at home or with.parish groups. Could you make an extra effort to celebrate Ash Wednesday together? Could you as a family join in the Holy Week liturgies? Could you promote a family discussion of values and how we form them? *St. Anthony Messenger's* special February 1977 issue about survival on our planet provides much material for discussions of Christian asceticism.

Could you read over the Sunday Scripture beforehand? Could your family undertake a common penance? a common work of charity? Like charity, penance begins at home. Fulfilling one's responsibility should have first claim on our energies; penance is not a reason to dodge those duties.

A Word of Caution

For all our creativeness in identifying more suitable forms of penance, an old and beguiling error may reappear: our external acts of penance might become more important than inner conversion. That was the mistake of many Pharisees in Jesus' time. Thus the man who self-righteously fasted twice a week was severely criticized by our Lord (Luke 18:14).

Our acts of penance could mislead us to think we are *earning* our salvation whereas we are *cooperating* with the free and absolutely-unmerited grace of God. Ultimately, the most penitential and saintly person among us is a faithful servant of the Lord who alone saves. Formalism (cold or blind observance without repentance) is always a possibility for us. Inner conversion to God's ways remains the heart of penance.

But penance is not a gloomy and oppressive duty for Christians. Jesus himself warned against looking sad when fasting (Matt. 6:16–18). Do our friends see us as joyful penitents? Do they

97

see men and women who know that Christ's death and resurrection have given a new meaning to the sufferings of this life? If our penance makes us gloomy and bitter, it is not from the Lord.

Does the Church still believe in penance? Definitely. Is Lent still a time of penance? Certainly. The Church has relaxed some of the penance she once legislated only to stress that inner conversion is essential to true penance. Whoever is convinced of the need for penance and knows its center (Christ crucified and risen) will, in all humility, find an appropriate penitential practice.

Questions for Discussion

1. What acts of penance, besides fasting and abstinence, does the Church urge Catholics to observe during Lent?

2. Why would it appear to some Catholics that the Church has given up on penance?

3. What role should prayer play in your penitential practice? How can you and your parish group make prayer a part of your daily routine?

4. What is the motive for fasting? What other acts of self-discipline can you practice during Lent?

5. What Lenten practices do you and your family observe/celebrate together?

Popular Devotions in Our Times

by Suzanne Molleur

Many older Catholics today are disturbed by what seems to them a loss of devotion in the Church. They see fewer people praying the rosary. They see Benediction services and novenas disappearing or poorly attended. They hear few sermons on the Sacred Heart—and even fewer hymns centered on this devotion. They find it hard to buy once-popular religious items like scapulars and Miraculous Medals. And in many churches the Stations of the Cross and statues so important to their private prayer have been banished or relegated to back corners.

Guitars and banners in church. Christian yoga. Christian zen. Charismatic prayer meetings. Bumper stickers. Masses that may seem to them zany or noisy or downright irreverent. Where, many ask, is the piety of earlier years?

The answer could be, "Right there." In the guitars and banners, yoga and zen, charismatic prayer meetings, bumper stickers and liturgy planning committees. Like friends of a mutual friend, two generations may be revealing their love differently, and who can say the mutual friend is more pleased with one expression of that love than another?

New Accent on Scripture

Perhaps most important among the changing aspects of Catholic spirituality is an increased emphasis on Scripture and liturgy. Once it was possible to be Catholic and have no more acquaintance with the Bible than the Gospels that were read year after year on Sunday. Mass was in Latin, Bible vigils were unknown, Scripture courses were few and far between. Because there was so little emphasis on Scripture and so little familiarity with it, many Catholics simply didn't read the Bible. And if they did, they were likely to find much of it incomprehensible.

Now more accurate and readable translations are available. The liturgy is completely in English, and a new three-year cycle has increased the number and variety of readings. The results of Catholic biblical scholarship have reached many, not only through new translations but through books, CCD, college and high school courses, magazine and newspaper features as well. In addition, much of the new religious music incorporates scriptural texts, sometimes almost verbatim.

Whether increased exposure to Scripture has led to increased interest, or whether increasing interest has generated greater exposure is a chicken-and-egg kind of question. But undoubtedly more Catholics read the Bible, and those who don't are becoming better acquainted with it in spite of themselves.

Thus, Scripture has become more significant in Catholic devotion. Time that might once have gone into saying the rosary or attending novenas may now, for some Catholics, be going into reading, studying or meditating on Scripture. And psalms or other scriptural passages may come more readily to their lips than the Memorare, Morning Offering or favorite prayers to a saint.

Stepped-Up Role of Liturgy

Liturgy, too, plays a larger role. Celebration of the Eucharist and sacraments in English allows the people to be drawn more deeply into their meaning and action. The newer flexibility in choice of readings and music and in use of drama, dance, audiovisual material, processions, etc., permits each Mass to speak to groups and occasions in a way not possible before. It also provides the opportunity and incentive for lay people to get involved in planning Masses.

With liturgical changes making greater participation and understanding possible, many Catholics find the Mass and sacraments newly satisfying means of encountering God, giving praise and adoration, seeking help and expressing their love. As the liturgical use of song, Scripture and prayer becomes more dominant in Catholic consciousness, it quite naturally becomes the model for other, non-liturgical services like Bible vigils, family celebrations, and modifications of older devotions like the rosary and Stations.

All this is in keeping with the teaching of Vatican Council II that "the liturgy is the summit toward which the activity of the Church is directed; at the same time it is the fountain from which all her power flows." The Mass, sacraments and Divine Office are, after all, the central acts of Catholic worship, the focus of all our devotion. What takes place there should generate, nourish and most perfectly express the love for God from which our spiritual life grows.

How Devotions Arise

So where does this leave devotions, public or private? We run here into a problem of definitions. What's the difference between *devotion* and *devotions*? Between *public* and *private* devotions? What relation do they have to the liturgy? What, for that matter, is the *liturgy*?

The liturgy is the official worship of the Church. In the Eucharist the Church reenacts Christ's redemptive sacrifice. In the sacraments it exercises his saving power. In the Divine

Office it prays his eternal prayer of praise to the Father. The liturgy is concerned above all with the central mysteries of our faith—with the dying, rising and eternal life of Jesus in the Father and with our sharing of their life through their Spirit of mutual love.

To explain the relationship between liturgy and devotions or between devotion and devotions, we could use an ordinary human family as our reference point. If I love my mother and father, I would be devoted to them. Because I love them, I would *want* to love them, want to please them, want to serve them in whatever way I could. And my brothers and sisters, if they had devotion, would do likewise.

Each of us, however, might channel that devotion differently. I might prefer to help with the housework. My brother might prefer to help in the yard. My sister might love to cook for them. Another sister could simply like being with them.

And the devotion of each of us could be prompted by different things. I might be motivated most by my father's tenderness and my mother's charm. My brother might respond more deeply to their never-failing patience with him. And my sister might be moved most by their years of care for her in her illness.

We each might have special affection for one or some of our parents' friends and relatives—people dear to them, people important in their lives and ours, people dear to us now in their own right. And with both friends and parents, our ways of showing our devotion and love might change through the years as we ourselves change, acquiring new insights, skills and interests.

Focus on a Central Love

In all of this, the central reality would be our parents, their mutual love for each other that made our existence possible, their loving will that we exist, and their constant, self-sacrificing care. This above all would merit celebration and reaffirmation, because in celebrating something we relive it and re-create

it; and without proper recognition of the primary things in
our lives, the secondary things can easily lose focus and get
distorted.

The central mysteries of God's triune life and love, revealed
in Jesus Christ, his Church, the Eucharist and the sacraments,
are the primary reality to which our love and life must respond.
Because the Father has loved us and sent his only-begotten
Son to become one with us, we can love God in his own spirit
of love. And if we love, we will have devotion.

But like children stirred by different aspects of their parents'
being and meaning, we may be moved by different aspects of
the one, incomprehensible reality we celebrate in the liturgy.
Like the son moved by his parents' never-failing patience,
some of us may be moved most by the Lord's never-failing
kindness and forgiveness. Like the daughter touched by her
parents' care for her in illness, some of us might find our
motivation in the Lord's answer to our helplessness and need.
Like children with a special affection for an aunt or family
friend, we may hold a special place in our hearts for Mary or a
saint.

Moved differently by different aspects of the one great mystery of God's love, we will find different ways of nurturing
and showing our love in return. Because we will have *devotion*,
we will practice *devotions*. Some—private devotions—we will
practice in our private prayer life or in small groups. Others—
public devotions like Benediction, group novenas, the Stations—
may take place in a church outside the liturgy.

Devotional Values — The Rosary

With all this in mind, let's look at some devotions popular in
the recent past and try to determine what value they've had
and can still have now and in the future. A good one to begin
with is the rosary.

For years the most widely practiced nonliturgical devotion in
the Western Church, the rosary has become a memory for
many Catholics who used to say it regularly or were surrounded

by friends and relatives who did. Many younger Catholics are not familiar with it at all.

As a repetition of one prayer addressed to Mary, it can easily lend itself to misunderstanding and misuse. People may attach undue value to the number of Hail Mary's said. Such an emphasis may be bound up with a mechanistic view of prayer as some kind of spiritual money which buys results—the more prayers or rosaries said, the better the chances. This in turn has often been bound up with a distorted view of Mary and God which sees the Lord as some kind of petty tyrant whose good will can best be gotten through the coaxing of a favorite servant.

Some of this has certainly turned some Catholics from the rosary. Others are simply turned off by what they experience

---

Piety Changes But Faith Doesn't

It is always important to remember that popular devotions do not exist for themselves. They exist to help us express and grow in our faith, hope, love, gratitude, acceptance of God's will, sorrow, admiration, and to honor God. The value of any particular devotion for any particular individual or group of people is related to its ability or effectiveness to do that.

History makes us aware that what moves people or best expresses their feelings toward God changes and varies with times, places and persons. Irish piety is different from Italian piety. The religious music and art of the Spanish differ markedly from the music and art of the Africans.

Until the time of St. Francis of Assisi, a royally-robed or priestly-robed Christ usually hung from the crucifix. St. Francis chose to emphasize the bleeding, pierced, suffering Jesus in a realistic figure on the cross. In the spirit of Francis his followers spread the devotion of the Way of the Cross over the whole world.

---

as the unrelieved monotony of saying one set of words over and over.

What is lost sight of in either case is the rosary's real power as a vehicle for interior prayer. The very repetitiveness of what is said—whether audibly or silently—frees the mind and spirit for prayer at a deeper level. The rhythm and sound of the words become part of one's whole being. I can choose to think about the prayer's meaning or that of the mysteries associated with each decade. On the other hand, I need not think at all, but simply be aware of God's presence at the center of my being, the sense of which is intensified by the vocal prayer. If my mind wanders or my concentration wavers, the words and physical reality of the beads are there to pull me back, to remind me of what I am about.

Later in the Middle Ages came the devotion of Forty Hours of adoration and honor given the exposed Blessed Sacrament.

In the 18th century Jesus' appearances to St. Margaret Mary Alacoque sparked a rebirth of piety expressed in devotion to the Sacred Heart, with the practice of receiving communion on the First Fridays of the month, enshrining and honoring the image of the Sacred Heart in homes, schools and churches.

Nearer our own time Fatima started the practice of communion and rosaries on First Saturdays.

Certain novenas or devotions to saints or our Lord or Mary took on special popularity in particular places. Interestingly enough, the rosary—introduced by the followers of St. Dominic into a Church already 1,200 years old—is hardly known in the Eastern Rite; the *Enchiridion of Indulgences* offers Eastern Rite Catholics a substitute way of obtaining a rosary indulgence. And the Jesus Prayer, so dear to Eastern Catholics, is just now becoming familiar to Latin Catholics.   —Norman Perry, O.F.M.

Similar forms of repetitive prayer and bead-counting are known in other religions throughout the world. The Catholic practice of repeating short phrases called aspirations or ejaculations embodies the same principles.

Whether in the rosary or ejaculations, the kind of prayer involved—while never a substitute for the liturgy—is valid and important. And in the case of the rosary, its Marian emphasis both fosters and expresses the devotion of those Catholics who are particularly inspired by the role of Mary in salvation.

Other Popular Devotions

The various Sacred Heart devotions nourish and express a devotion centered in the real humanity of the love experienced by the person Jesus. Making the First Fridays isn't—or shouldn't be—a magic formula for entering into heaven but a way of drawing us to reflect on and enter through the Mass into this aspect of the Incarnation. Novenas, consecrations, acts of reparation needn't—and shouldn't—be empty gestures, things to do because they sound good or satisfy a sense of duty or guilt or guarantee a desired response to some petition. Rather, they can be instruments of prayer through which we see into and experience more deeply the mystery of One who shares our human heart and knows what it is to love with a human love.

Similarly, I venerate the Eucharist in Benediction because I am devoted to the Lord's Real Presence, and in entering into its meaning again through Benediction my devotion is renewed. Or in making the Stations regularly I both show my response to the Lord's passion and death and strengthen it, because if I am truly reflecting on the meaning of each station, truly entering into his suffering, truly letting that suffering speak to me about my own sinfulness and weakness, then my desire to respond in love must increase.

Why the Decline?

Every devotional practice is valuable in much the same way.

Why, then, have so many well-known devotions declined in popularity in recent years?

Partially because of misguided eagerness in implementing changes called for by Vatican II. Partially because of changes in living habits in an on-the-go modern society with too much to do, see and choose from. Partially from changes in values, behavioral styles, ways of doing and seeing and understanding things. Partially from reaction to the undue importance sometimes given devotions in a pre-Vatican-Council, Latin-liturgy Church where devotions were the only things people could actually participate in or experience without the need for explanation or translation.

It's hard to trace cause and effect precisely. Where people are involved in changes of vast proportions, many causes come together to create many effects, and what holds true for one Catholic may not hold true at all for another. Even in an age of religious stability and uniformity, not everyone will practice the same devotions, because we are individuals with different histories, life-styles and temperaments.

Which Way Popular Devotion?

For some Catholics things like yoga and zen provide the same kind of avenue into deep interior prayer that the rosary has provided many others. For charismatic Catholics prayer in tongues is similarly important. In an age of confusion and rapid change the ordering and creative work of the Holy Spirit is an aspect of the faith to which more and more people are responding. And much more than in the recent past, literature, film, photography and other art forms are becoming devotional matter through use in prayer, liturgy and nonliturgical celebrations.

It is always important to remember that popular devotions do not exist for themselves. The value of particular devotions for any individual or group is related to their effectiveness in nourishing and expressing *devotion*.

So if some of us find the devotions of our youth no longer

109

being practiced by our children, we shouldn't be disturbed because *our* devotions are not being practiced. The mere fact of change should not be alarming. What we may find regrettable is the fact that devotions are discarded or ignored because they have never been properly explained. The fact that devotions like the rosary, Way of the Cross, meditation on the Sacred Heart, prayer and novenas to Mary and the saints have been fruitful for many generations of Catholics is reason enough for wanting all Catholics to at least be acquainted with them, their theology and their proper use.

If after that, some Catholics protest that traditional devotions are not helpful to *them*, we shouldn't be shocked or scandalized. What matters, in the end, is that every Catholic have a living, growing devotion, without which all the devotional practices in the world are meaningless.

Questions for Discussion

1. What is the difference between *devotion* and *devotions*? What is *liturgy*?

2. What does the author say is the rosary's "real power as a vehicle for prayer"? What value do other popular devotions have?

3. What factors are responsible for the decline in devotions?

4. How has the Church's increased emphasis on Scripture and liturgy affected Catholic devotions?

5. How have changes in the liturgy made greater participation and easier understanding possible?

About the Authors

Mary Ann Deak was graduated in 1970 from Edgecliff College in Cincinnati. She has been active in lay missionary work, serving as a volunteer in Kentucky for one year, and has taught catechetics. She recently joined the Glenmary Sisters, headquartered in Cincinnati.

George Alliger has an M.A. in theology from Mt. St. Mary of the West Seminary in Cincinnati. He is a member of the New Jerusalem Catholic charismatic community in the same city.

Jack Wintz, O.F.M., was ordained in 1963. Holding an M.A. in English literature from Xavier University in Cincinnati, he has been an English teacher and writer for several years both in the U.S. and the Philippines. He is the editor of the *Catholic Update* series and an associate editor of *St. Anthony Messenger.*

Leonard Foley, O.F.M., associate editor of *St. Anthony Messenger* and editor of *Homily Helps* for priests, has had varied experience as teacher, parish priest and retreat master. His books include *Your Confession: Using the New Ritual, Signs of Love: The Sacraments of Christ, Saint of the Day* and *Sincerely Yours, Paul.*

111

Barbara Beckwith is an assistant editor of *St. Anthony Messenger* and has a B.A. in journalism from Marquette University in Milwaukee, Wisconsin. Previously she worked as news editor for a weekly newspaper in Wisconsin.

Karen Hurley is an assistant editor of *St. Anthony Messenger* and holds an M.A. in theology from the University of Notre Dame. She has taught religion at a Catholic high school, and religious studies to adults and college students in Williamsburg, Virginia.

Patrick McCloskey, O.F.M., was ordained in June, 1975, and is presently teaching at Roger Bacon High School in Cincinnati. He writes a monthly column for *St. Anthony Messenger* and is the author of *St. Anthony of Padua: Wisdom for Today*.

Suzanne Molleur was formerly an assistant editor of *St. Anthony Messenger*. A graduate of Lowell State College, Lowell, Massachusetts, with a B.A. in English, she has also worked in advertising and city government. She is presently in a postulancy program at the Carmelite Monastery in Indianapolis, considering entering the contemplative life.